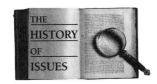

THE
HISTORY
OF
ISSUES

Violence in the Media

D1040712

Other Books in the History of Issues Series:

Violence in the Media

Jodie Lynn Boduch, Book Editor

GREENHAVEN PRESS

An imprint of Thomson Gale, a part of The Thomson Corporation

Detroit • New York • San Francisco • New Haven, Conn. • Waterville, Maine • London

Christine Nasso, *Publisher*
Elizabeth Des Chenes, *Managing Editor*

© 2008 The Gale Group.

Star logo is a trademark and Gale and Greenhaven Press are registered trademarks used herein under license.

For more information, contact:
Greenhaven Press
27500 Drake Rd.
Farmington Hills, MI 48331-3535
Or you can visit our Internet site at http://www.gale.com

ALL RIGHTS RESERVED
No part of this work covered by the copyright hereon may be reproduced or used in any form or by any means—graphic, electronic, or mechanical, including photocopying, record-ing, taping, Web distribution, or information storage retrieval systems—without the written permission of the publisher.

Articles in Greenhaven Press anthologies are often edited for length to meet page require-ments. In addition, original titles of these works are changed to clearly present the main thesis and to explicitly indicate the author's opinion. Every effort is made to ensure that Greenhaven Press accurately reflects the original intent of the authors. Every effort has been made to trace the owners of copyrighted material.

Cover photograph reproduced by permission of © K. & H. Benser/zefa/Corbis.

ISBN-13: 978-0-7377-2875-0 (hardcover)
ISBN-10: 0-7377-2875-2 (hardcover)

2007939022

Contents

Chapter 3: Media Violence in the 1990s and Beyond

Foreword

In the 1940s, at the height of the Holocaust, Jews struggled to create a nation of their own in Palestine, a region of the Middle East that at the time was controlled by Britain. The British had placed limits on Jewish immigration to Palestine, hampering efforts to provide refuge to Jews fleeing the Holocaust. In response to this and other British policies, an underground Jewish resistance group called Irgun began carrying out terrorist attacks against British targets in Palestine, including immigration, intelligence, and police offices. Most famously, the group bombed the King David Hotel in Jerusalem, the site of a British military headquarters. Although the British were warned well in advance of the attack, they failed to evacuate the building. As a result, ninety-one people were killed (including fifteen Jews) and forty-five were injured.

Early in the twentieth century, Ireland, which had long been under British rule, was split into two countries. The south, populated mostly by Catholics, eventually achieved independence and became the Republic of Ireland. Northern Ireland, mostly Protestant, remained under British control. Catholics in both the north and south opposed British control of the north, and the Irish Republican Army (IRA) sought unification of Ireland as an independent nation. In 1969 the IRA split into two factions. A new radical wing, the Provisional IRA, was created and soon undertook numerous terrorist bombings and killings throughout Northern Ireland, the Republic of Ireland, and even in England. One of its most notorious attacks was the 1974 bombing of a Birmingham, England, bar that killed nineteen people.

In the mid-1990s an Islamic terrorist group called al Qaeda began carrying out terrorist attacks against American targets overseas. In communications to the media, the organization listed several complaints against the United States. It generally opposed all U.S. involvement and presence in the Middle East. It particularly objected to the presence of U.S. troops in Saudi Arabia, which is the home of several Islamic holy sites. And it strongly condemned the United States for supporting the nation of Israel, which it claimed was an oppressor of Muslims. In 1998 al Qaeda's leaders issued a fatwa (a religious legal statement) calling for Muslims to kill Americans. Al Qaeda acted on this order many times—most memorably on September 11, 2001, when it attacked the World Trade Center and the Pentagon, killing nearly three thousand people.

These three groups—Irgun, the Provisional IRA, and al Qaeda—have achieved varied results. Irgun's terror campaign contributed to Britain's decision to pull out of Palestine and to support the creation of Israel in 1948. The Provisional IRA's tactics kept pressure on the British, but they also alienated many would-be supporters of independence for Northern Ireland. Al Qaeda's attacks provoked a strong U.S. military response but did not lessen America's involvement in the Middle East nor weaken its support of Israel. Despite these different results, the means and goals of these groups were similar. Although they emerged in different parts of the world during different eras and in support of different causes, all three had one thing in common: They all used clandestine violence to undermine a government they deemed oppressive or illegitimate.

The destruction of oppressive governments is not the only goal of terrorism. For example, terror is also used to minimize dissent in totalitarian regimes and to promote extreme ideologies. However, throughout history the motivations of terrorists have been remarkably similar, proving the old adage that "the more things change, the more they remain the same." Arguments for and against terrorism thus boil down to the same set of universal arguments regardless of the age: Some argue that terrorism is justified to change (or, in the case of state terror, to maintain) the prevailing political order; others respond that terrorism is inhumane and unacceptable under any circumstances. These basic views transcend time and place.

Similar fundamental arguments apply to other controversial social issues. For instance, arguments over the death penalty have always featured competing views of justice. Scholars cite biblical texts to claim that a person who takes a life must forfeit his or her life, while others cite religious doctrine to support their view that only God can take a human life. These arguments have remained essentially the same throughout the centuries. Likewise, the debate over euthanasia has persisted throughout the history of Western civilization. Supporters argue that it is compassionate to end the suffering of the dying by hastening their impending death; opponents insist that it is society's duty to make the dying as comfortable as possible as death takes its natural course.

Greenhaven Press's The History of Issues series illustrates this constancy of arguments surrounding major social issues. Each volume in the series focuses on one issue—including terrorism, the death penalty, and euthanasia—and examines how the debates have both evolved and remained essentially the same over the years. Primary documents such as newspaper articles, speeches, and government reports illuminate historical developments and offer perspectives from throughout history. Secondary sources provide overviews and commentaries from a more contemporary perspective. An introduction begins each anthology and supplies essential context and background. An annotated table of contents, chronology, and index allow for easy reference, and a bibliography and list of organizations to contact point to additional sources of information on the book's topic. With these features, The History of Issues series permits readers to glimpse both the historical and contemporary dimensions of humanity's most pressing and controversial social issues.

Introduction

Violence as public spectacle is not a modern phenomenon; a glimpse back at the gladiatorial contests of ancient Rome proves it. However, the rise of mass media in the past century or so has meant more outlets for the societal consumption of violence—in the form of entertainment, sensational news, or current events. During this same period, there has also been an increase in the violent crime rate. The reality of more people subject to more violence in ever-broader forms of media has provoked a challenging social issues debate over this question: Does violence in the media influence those who are exposed to it?

One might wonder what triggered this question in the first place. Psychologists Brad J. Bushman and Craig A. Anderson posit that "[O]ne reason for the early interest in a link between media violence and societal violence is that violence in the United States began to increase fairly dramatically in 1965, exactly when the first generation of children raised on TV began to reach the prime ages for committing violent crimes."[1] Another reason turns the clock back even further to the 1930s, when the Payne Fund Studies delved into the question for purely academic reasons: To determine whether there were any social effects of the then-novel mass visual media (motion pictures).

As with any controversial issue, there are no simple or straightforward answers. Defining media violence, exploring what kind of influence it has and how, gauging who is influenced, and understanding what actions have been taken regarding media violence are the initial steps toward understanding the issue.

Definitions

Defining media violence is an easy task at first glance. "Media" consists of print publications (including comic books), television (both news and entertainment), films, animation, video games, music and other audio communications, and computer or internet-based media.

"Violence" is more difficult to define. Indeed, the lack of precise measures as to what constitutes violence, or how certain things should be "weighted," has contributed to the overall debate. Some acts or images of violence are graphic and indisputable, such as someone shooting or stabbing someone else at close range. Other acts or images are more difficult to classify, such as pushing. And is violence always physical, or should depictions of psychological or emotional harm or suffering also be considered in the media violence debate? The blurred lines of what is and is not violence add to the complexity of the issue and help explain why a variety of positions exist.

What Kind of Influence?

The notion of "influence" in this context has several meanings. The first meaning, and the one that serves as the underlying assumption for most discussions about violence in the media, concerns psychological effects. A great deal of scientific research has been performed (and continues to be conducted) in order to assess what, if any, links there are between exposure to media violence and its impact on individuals at the emotional, social, and behavioral levels. The fundamental thread is discerning the connection between media violence and aggressive thoughts or feelings and again between aggressive thoughts or feelings and violent action.

Public opinion is another area affected by violence in the media. Violent imagery or written descriptions of current events may strike a chord with the community at large. For example, in late nineteenth-century London, sensational news coverage of the Jack the Ripper murders triggered fear among the city's inhabitants; it also renewed a cultural discussion about socioeconomic class differences and social welfare. Another example of media violence and public opinion involves newsreel footage of war or terrorist acts, which, in a democratic society, may indirectly shape foreign policy: Viewers may form opinions on foreign or public policy based on what they see, and they make take these opinions with them to the voting booths and seek to elect political leaders accordingly.

There is a lack of consensus as to the extent of media violence influence, especially in the realm of psychological effects. It is precisely this inability to agree that has shaped much of the debate on the media violence issue.

How Does Media Violence Influence People?

The lack of consensus as to whether or not violence in the media renders psychological effects is due, at least in part, by the uncertainty as to *how* it influences people. A variety of factors must be weighed when attempting to assess the "how," and because many of them are subjective, it once again becomes difficult to quantify. For example, the nature or severity of the violence is no doubt of importance, but individuals perceive violence differently. What may seem especially intense for one person may seem less severe for another. Likewise, the matter of frequency might also impact how media violence is received: Will one exposure have an effect or will it take multiple exposures? A parallel question explores the reverse: Is there a point at which an individual can become "desensitized" to violence in the media? Finally, the lingering effects component should also be examined: If one is influenced by media violence, are those effects permanent or do they "wear off" after a period of time? These sorts of questions, many of which are subjective, add to the complex nature of the issue.

A study aiming to examine whether there is a correlation between violent song lyrics and aggression illustrates these points. After a series of five psychological experiments in which they concluded that there is, in fact, a correlation, the authors insist that "research on potential violent song effects on aggressive behavior becomes even more important now that we have clearly demonstrated that such songs increase aggressive thoughts and feelings."[2] However, the authors add, it is probable that the observed effects of violent song lyrics might be short-lasting. They also indicate that song lyrics are often experienced secondarily because the listener is often engaged in another activity. Nevertheless, the researchers expect this less-studied aspect of the media violence issue to derive similar results as its visual counterparts: "There are now good theoretical and empirical reasons to expect effects of music lyrics on aggressive behavior to be similar to the well-studied effects of exposure to TV and movie violence and the more recent research on video games."[3]

Whom Does It Influence?

One reason the issue of violence in the media is such a topic is because of the population most susceptible to its effects: children. In fact, most of the research conducted—both government-sponsored and privately funded—has been on children. While there is little agreement about the extent or how media violence affects children, there is no dispute that any potential influence has an impact on this group above all others. One group of scholars in the field of pediatrics reminds us that in the United States, children and adolescents spend more time engaged in media activities than any other activity (with the exception of sleeping).[4] Because children respond to psychological stimulus more actively than adults, and because children are powerless to make societal changes in the way adults can, the media violence issue has become a public health debate as well.

Adults, too, may be influenced by media violence, especially violence that impacts the general public. Less research is devoted to the psychological impact of media violence on adults, but this aspect has not been ignored and still factors into the debate.

What Actions Have Been Taken?

The public health and other social concerns about violence in the media have garnered more than just discussion and debate about the issue. As mentioned, both the U.S. government and private institutions have sponsored social science research initiatives in order to arrive at more concrete answers. In addition, a number of nonprofit organizations have been established to raise awareness about media violence. Some professional organizations, such as the American Medical Association, American Academy of Pediatrics, and American Psychological Association, have issued guidelines for practitioners and educational brochures summarizing research findings or offering practical tips to which the findings apply. The American Psychological Association's policy manual includes a section on television violence as it affects children. The statement was adopted in 1985 after a published study supported by the National Institute of Mental Health and notes the following:

> BE IT RESOLVED that the American Psychological Association (1) encourages parents to monitor and to control television viewing by children; (2) requests industry representatives to take a responsible attitude in reducing direct imitatable violence on "real-life" fictional children's programming or violent incidents on cartoons, and in providing more programming for children designed to mitigate possible effects of television violence, consistent with the guarantees of the First Amendment; and (3) urges industry, government, and private foundations to support relevant research activities aimed at the amelioration of the effects of high levels of televised violence on children's attitudes and behaviors.[5]

The issue has also prompted political movements, with groups forming to advocate support or opposition to laws aiming to regulate or control media violence within the entertainment industry (including television, films, music, and videogames).

Responsibility

If one side of the media violence coin is influence and effects, the other is responsibility. On the question of ultimate responsibility for media violence content and its potential effects, fingers have been pointed—to greater and lesser degrees—at the entertainment industry, the government, parents, and society in general. As the most often-cited target of media violence critiques, the entertainment industry has been variously encouraged to self-regulate and, in some cases, required to adhere to federal laws (e.g., ratings labels on television shows, films, music, and videogames). Yet controversy exists here, too, concerning free speech and other factors not related to the media violence-psychological effects link.

In 1997, Professors George Gerbner and Todd Gitlin engaged in a public debate on the question of whether media violence constitutes free speech. Gerbner argued that entertainment media violence is not an expression of crime statistics or freedom but rather a marketing instrument of fear and social control: He noted that the Cultural Indicators Project found that frequent viewers of media violence had a greater sense of insecurity and mistrust than those who viewed less frequently. Gitlin claimed the opposite. His position was that there was no direct link between entertainment violence and physical violence—such a view, he says, is a politically convenient tool—but that instead it was an example of cultural low-browed banality. It's "stupid," he said, not "dangerous." In essence, both professors see problems with media violence for reasons—free speech, cultural impact, method of control—that go beyond the link between exposure and aggression.[6]

Questions, Answers, and More Questions

Clearly, the issue of violence in the media is a rich topic not likely to subside in the near future. Because so much of what comprises the subject—definitions, measuring and determining effects, actions to be taken or not taken—contains gray areas, some questions may never have answers agreed upon by everyone. Some observers cite not only the gray areas themselves, but also the manner in which news outlets have covered the debate as a complicating factor. Bushman and Anderson maintain that "[R]easons for this discontinuity between news reports and the actual state of scientific knowledge include the vested interest of the news, a misapplied fairness doctrine in news reporting, and the failure of the research community to effectively argue the scientific case."[7] Research and discussion about the issue has been productive insofar as *more* questions arise, giving the media violence debate additional dimensions. The more insight that can be gleaned, the better informed society can be when making decisions relevant to this issue.

Notes

1. Bushman, B.A., & Anderson, C. A. (2001). "Media Violence and the American Public: Scientific Fact Versus Media Misinformation." *American Psychologist, 56*(6/7), 477.
2. Anderson, C. A., Carnagey, N., & Eubanks, J. (2003): "Exposure to Violent Media: The Effects of Songs with Violent Lyrics on Aggressive Thoughts and Feelings." *Journal of Personality and Social Psychology, 84*(5), 969.
3. Ibid.
4. Cheng, T.L., Brenner, R. A., Wright, J. L., Sachs, H. C., Moyer, P., & Rao, M.R. (2004). "Children's Violent Television Viewing: Is Anyone Watching?" *Pediatrics, 114*(1), 94–99.
5. "APA Resolution XXXIII (Violence)" (1985). *American Psychological Association, Council Policy Manual: N. Public Interest, Part 5*. Available from http://www.apa.org/about/division/cpmpubint5.html#33.
6. "Is Media Violence Free Speech? A Debate between George Gerbner and Todd Gitlin." (1997). *Hot Wired*. Available from http://www.media-awareness.ca/english/resources/articles/violence/violence_speech.cfm?
7. Bushman & Anderson, "Media Violence and the American Public," 478.

CHAPTER 1

The Origins of Media Violence Issues

Chapter Preface

Violence as entertainment is not a modern phenomenon. History is littered with examples of public spectacles with violence-for-pleasure as the central theme, and critics of violent entertainment appear alongside these examples. Sissela Bok writes about the parallels between gladiator games in ancient Rome and the twentieth-century birth of violence on film and television. Among the few critics were early Christians, who were on the margins of Roman society at the time. They neither clung to the prevailing culture of violence nor had their critiques taken seriously.

Violence in the news is also a trend with pre-twentieth century roots. L. Perry Curtis explains how newspaper coverage of the Jack the Ripper murders in London during the late 1880s affected public opinion. According to Curtis, the murder news—often sensationally and graphically depicted—served to sell papers as well as to lecture readers about societal norms. This early glimpse into the influence of mass media hints at the underpinnings of media violence questions posed several decades later.

The dawn of film-making in the early twentieth century was a key turning point in American pop culture. The new media brought with it curiosity on many fronts, including that of the social sciences. In the 1930s, the Payne Fund studies began an exploration of the social impact of motion pictures. W. W. Charters' study concluded that movies produced a more intense impact on children than on adults. Given their ability to influence adults and, especially, children, Charters said, movies should be used in a more positive manner.

Researchers continued their interest in the social effects of mass media, with the advent of television introducing yet another avenue of inquiry. Frederic Wertham devoted his scholarship to the psychologically harmful impact of media violence on children. In the 1960s, he suggested that media such as films, television, and comic books were potentially harmful because they taught violence as a means of conflict resolution.

All social issues begin somewhere, and the topics mentioned here provide a few pieces of the origins puzzle. Reviewing the foundations of violent spectacles and their social consequences allows us to understand the evolution of the media violence debate.

Violence as Spectacle in Ancient Rome

Sissela Bok

*In the following selection, Sissela Bok traces the origins of vio-
lence as entertainment to Ancient Roman society. She describes
the Roman appetite for spectacles of violence as manifested
through gladiator battles both at private banquets and in public
arenas. Such battles to the death, Bok notes, had many celebrants but few critics, with the exception of the philosopher
Seneca and some early Christians (who were cultural outsiders
to Roman society). The author believes that fear, profiteering,
and an overall culture of violence may explain why lethal games
for viewing pleasure had few challengers.*

*Bok suggests that contemporary assessments of Roman prac-
tices regarding violent entertainment should be kept in check by
an evaluation of modern norms about violence in the entertainment industry. She urges us not to overlook the modern-day parallels, even if they are uncomfortable.*

*Bok has a Ph.D. in philosophy and is Distinguished Fellow
at the Harvard Center for Population and Development Studies.
Her work involves commentary on ethical issues in government,
media, and public life. She is the author of four books.*

No people before or since have so reveled in displays of
mortal combat as did the Romans during the last two
centuries B.C. and the first three centuries thereafter, nor derived such pleasure from spectacles in which slaves and con-
victs were exposed to wild beasts and killed in front of cheering spectators. According to Nicolaus of Damascus, writing in
the first decade A.D., Romans even regaled themselves with lethal violence at private banquets; he describes dinner guests
relishing the spectacle of gladiators fighting to the death:

Sissela Bok, *Mayhem: Violence as Public Entertainment.* Reading, MA: Addison-Wesley,
1998, pp. 15–20, 22–23. Copyright © 1998 by Sissela Bok. Reprinted by permission of
Da Capo Press, a member of Perseus Books Group.

Hosts would invite their friends to dinner not merely for other entertainment, but that they might witness two or three pairs of contestants in a gladiatorial combat; on these occasions, when sated with dining and drink, they called in the gladiators. No sooner did one have his throat cut than the masters applauded with delight at this feat.

Violence at Close Hand

Perhaps the delectation and thrill of viewing a fight to the death at such close hand while reclining after a meal with friends provided even greater pleasure than the vast gladiatorial shows in the amphitheater, where thousands of combatants confronted death each year. Devotees versed in the aesthetics of violence and the "science of pleasure" could study at close hand the subtleties of the moves in each encounter and celebrate the nobility and beauty with which defeated gladiators who had been denied a reprieve bared their necks for decapitation.

The satiric poet Juvenal's phrase "bread and circuses"— *panem et circenses*—that has come down, through the centuries, to stand for public offerings of nourishment and spectacles on a grand scale, would have meant nothing to the earliest Romans. There is no evidence from their period of vast wild beast hunts in circuses or spectacular forms of capital punishment or gladiatorial combats to the death in the arena. The first gladiatorial fight we know of took place in 264 B.C., when the ex-consul Iunius Brutus Pera and his brother, in a ceremony to honor their dead father, presented three pairs of gladiators in the ox market. More such encounters were offered in the ensuing decades by private citizens as a way to honor dead relatives. But gladiatorial combat was increasingly seen, too, as entertainment and as evidence of generosity, even lavishness on the part of public officials.

Violent Spectacles

Barely two centuries after the first gladiatorial fights, they had become the centerpiece of the Roman "games," alongside wild animal hunts with live game brought from every corner of the known world to be slaughtered, and countless slaves, prisoners, and other victims "thrown to the beasts." Those who died thus were seen either as expendable nonhumans, such as slaves or wild beasts, as criminals or prisoners of war who justly deserved their fate, or as volunteers who had chosen to take part freely or sold themselves into service as gladiators.

Violent spectacles kept the citizenry distracted, engaged, and entertained and, along with reenactments and celebrations of conquests and sacrifices abroad, provided the continued acculturation to violence needed by a warrior state. And the association with bread was constant. Not only were shows in the amphitheater or the circus meant for feasting the eye as well as the emotions: many sponsors also gave out bread, meat, drink, and favorite dishes to the crowds gathered for the games. Elements of entertainment and feasting were combined with ritual and sacrifice. Ancient Rome seems a particularly striking illustration of the claim by literary scholar René Girard that all communal violence can be described in terms of sacrifice, using surrogate victims as means to protect the entire community against its own internal violence. No program could begin without a sacrifice to a deity, often Diana, who presided over the raucous hunting scenes, or Mars, patron of the gladiatorial combats; and after the bloodshed was over, "a figure, representing the powers of the under-world, gave the finishing stroke to the wretches who were still lingering."

Legitimate Violence

Throughout, such violence was regarded as legitimate, fully authorized, even commanded at the highest level of Roman society. The festive atmosphere, the rousing music of the bands, the chanting by the crowds, the betting on who would triumph or lose, the colorful costumes, and the adulation of star gladiators all contributed to the glamour attached to the games. But as historian Kathleen Coleman points out, while "the 'contagion of the throng' may aptly describe the thrill that the Roman spectators experienced in the Colosseum, [it] does not explain why their communal reaction was pleasure instead of revulsion or horror." Part of the reason, she suggests, is that the Roman world "was permeated by violence that had to be absorbed."

Just as Roman spectacles remain the prototype for violent entertainment at its most extreme, so Rome's own history illustrates the development of a prototypical "culture of violence." It was one in which violence was widely sanctioned and hallowed by tradition, in foreign conquest as in domestic culture; in which courage and manhood were exalted and weapons easily available; and in which the climate of brutality and callousness extended from the treatment of newborns and slaves in many homes to the crucifixions and other brutal punishments so common for noncitizens. Entertainment violence officially sponsored on a mass basis served to enhance every one of these aspects of Rome's martial culture.

Among Romans, spectacles of violence had many celebrants and few outspoken challengers. The poet Martial, in his *De Spectaculis*, written in A.D. 80 for the inauguration of the Colosseum, conveyed the magnificence of the fights and wild beast hunts in evocative tones. Speaking of a condemned criminal who, "hanging on no unreal cross gave up his vitals to a Caledonian bear," Martial described his mangled limbs as still living, "though the parts dripped gore, and in all his body was nowhere a body's shape. A punishment deserved at length he won." This death was staged as a performance of the story of Laureolus, a famous bandit leader who had been captured and crucified. This was a favorite subject for dramatic enactment, but as Martial pointed out, the victim in this instance was "hanging on no unreal cross," and his agony was compounded by exposure to the bear.

Few Critics

Why did such spectacles have so few outspoken critics among Romans? We can only wonder at the silence of those, like Marcus Aurelius and Epictetus, who proclaimed Stoic and other ideals of goodness and justice; not to mention the many other philosophers, poets, and legal scholars who were openly admiring of the practice. Like most Romans, they may have been too thoroughly acculturated to violence to see any need for criticism. The historian Tacitus recounts that "there are the peculiar and characteristic vices of this metropolis of ours, taken on, it seems to me, almost in the mother's womb—the passion for play actors and the mania for gladiatorial shows and horse-racing." At home as in the lecture halls, the gossip is all about such spectacles; even the teachers dwell largely on such material in their classes.

Along with such acculturation, fear was the great silencer of outrage and free debate among the Romans and the peoples they conquered. It was dangerous to speak freely, above all to criticize acts of the emperor and practices linked to his worship. At his whim, critics could be jailed, exiled, or thrown to the lions. But more than acculturation and fear was involved. Opportunistic self-censorship was rampant. Many among the intelligentsia and in the aristocracy derived great prestige from sponsoring displays of gladiators. They had a vested interest in seeing the games continue and in deriding criticism.

One who did note a moral paradox in the gladiatorial games presenting violence as public entertainment was the philosopher Seneca. He pointed to Pompey, reputedly conspicuous among leaders of the state for the kindness of his heart, who had been the first

> to exhibit the slaughter of eighteen elephants in the circus, pitting criminals against them in a mimic battle [and]

thought it a notable kind of spectacle to kill human beings after a new fashion. Do they fight to the death? That is not enough! Are they torn to pieces? That is not enough! Let them be crushed by animals of monstrous bulk!

Moral Paradox

That human beings should kill and maim their fellows was hardly paradoxical in its own right; rather, the oddity was that the pleasure in seeing it carried out could be so relished as to override all sense of respect for life: "Man, an object of reverence in the eyes of men, is now slaughtered for jest and sport ... and it is a satisfying spectacle to see a man made a corpse." For Seneca, sharing the enjoyment of that spectacle brutalized and desensitized viewers and fostered their appetite for still more cruelty. It undercut the central task of seeking to grow in humanity, in nobility of spirit, in understanding, and in freedom from greed, cruelty, and other desires; and thereby to progress toward self-mastery. Seneca saw *any* diversion as deflecting from this task; but taking pleasure in brutality—in "seeing a man made a corpse"—actually reversed the development, destroyed *humanitas,* the respectful kindness that characterizes persons who have learned how to be fully human among humans. Violent entertainments rendered spectators *crudelior et inhumanior*—"more cruel and more inhumane"— acculturating them to pitilessness and to lack of respect for their fellow humans and other creatures.

The same forces that numbed most Romans' shame or sense of moral paradox inherent in relishing such cruelty— acculturation, fear, and profiteering—also helped to dampen criticism in the provinces. Many Roman military encampments had their own amphitheaters, and hundreds of others were built for the public around the Empire in the first centuries A.D. But though Roman authorities and commercial sponsors encouraged attendance at the games in conquered territories as a form of homage to the emperor-deities, such spectacles could not compete in extravagance with those offered by the emperors in Rome and rarely met with the special exultation elsewhere that they evoked there. A few spoke out against them openly: when King Herod wished to offer spectacles in an amphitheater he had constructed near Jerusalem, "the Jews found such a cruel pleasure to be impious and an abandonment of their ancestral customs."

Early Christian Critics

Among the severest critics were Christians, from whose ranks so many were tortured and killed at the games. Late in the second century, Bishop Tertullian thundered . . . against violent spectacles rooted in pagan religion, with their brutalizing effects on victims, sponsors, combatants, and spectators alike. He lambasted the Christians who took pleasure in such shows and cautioned against the degradation that came, not just from viewing cruelty but from delighting in it, finding it entertaining, developing a "passion for murderous pleasure." With puritanical zeal, he insisted that people should avoid not only violent shows but all spectacles:

> There is no public spectacle without violence to the spirit. For where there is pleasure, there is eagerness, which gives pleasure its flavor. Where there is eagerness, there is rivalry, which gives its flavor to eagerness. Yes, and then, where there is rivalry, there also are madness, bile, anger, pain, and all the things that follow from them and (like them) are incompatible with moral discipline. . . .

Roman Practices Versus Today

Revulsion against the Roman gladiatorial games intensified during the third century. By the fourth, they had become for many what one historian calls "an unthinkable monstrosity." But even though they were outlawed again and again, they would flare up each time, until they were finally abolished for good in 438. Ever since, historians of the period have spoken of the chasm that separates us from the Romans in this regard. Keith Hopkins refers to the games, with their "welter of blood in gladiatorial and wild-beast shows, the squeals of the victims and of slaughtered animals," as "completely alien to us and almost unimaginable"; and Samuel Dill stresses our difficulty in conceiving of the fascination that the spectacles in the amphitheater and the theater had, "not only on characters hardened by voluptuousness, but on the cultivated and humane."

Just how unimaginable are the Roman practices to today's publics? Most people would recoil from the thought of banquets such as those described at the beginning of this chapter, offering guests the chance to feast not only on food and drink but also on gladiatorial combat. Even so, they might recognize the emotions underlying the guests' delight in viewing such fights at close hand and their aesthetic appreciation of the combatants' skill.

As we strive to understand in what sense the Roman practices might nevertheless be "completely alien" to us, we have to ask whether our contemporary versions of entertainment violence exhibit anything like the paradox inherent in the role of the gladiatorial games as public entertainment. This is not to say that our societies are at any risk of tolerating public spectacles such as Rome's. Our laws prohibit them, and our institutions allow the open debate and criticism that Romans could not have. Rather, what matters for us is to explore the uncomfortable present-day parallels to the thrill and joyful entertainment associated with watching bloodshed, the function of the games in acculturating the Romans to violence, and the exploiting of even the bloodthirstiest practices by Rome's commercial and political vested interests, not to mention the self-censorship practiced by man of its authors, artists, and critics.

Murder News as Cultural Event in Victorian England

L. Perry Curtis Jr.

The following excerpt from the introduction to L. Perry Curtis Jr.'s book Jack the Ripper and the London Press *evaluates media coverage of Jack the Ripper, a serial killer whose crimes against five prostitutes terrorized the East End of London in 1888.*

Curtis maintains that the way the press covered the crimes reflected the fears and concerns of Victorian society. Mass circulation daily newspapers, themselves an emerging phenomenon in late nineteenth-century London, played a role in shaping public opinion. By engaging in graphically detailed reporting that fascinated the public, some newspapers served to inform as well as to sermonize about the "danger to law and order" the Ripper murders presented. According to Curtis, other papers sensationalized the case as a means of commenting on social conditions in the East End of London. Curtis concludes that because much remained unknown about the unsolved Ripper case, newspapers filled in the blanks with speculation and editorial asides.

Curtis is professor Emeritus of History and Modern Media and Culture at Brown University. He is the author of two books and numerous articles on Victorian history and culture.

My study of murder news is . . . concerned with "them"— namely, the Victorians who wrote and read all those lurid articles about the Whitechapel horrors and who felt the panics, shocks, and thrills arising therefrom. The core chapters herein deal with newspaper texts as though they were ideologically charged and fragmented images of events that had

L. Perry Curtis Jr., *Jack the Ripper and the London Press*. New Haven, CT: Yale University Press, 2001, pp. 8–15. Copyright © 2001 by Yale University. All rights reserved. Reproduced by permission.

passed through the filters of witnesses, reporters, editors, and, of course, readers, all of whom carried their own preconceptions. The distorting effects of all this filtering prevent us from ever attaining a complete grasp of the original events, despite the apparent authority of each newspaper account. Equally important, reporters often devoted some time and space to their own surmises and rumors gleaned from contacts or witnesses. In other words, all the unknowns in these murders created a thousand and one openings for imaginations to run riot. Whether by means of feature articles, leaders, or letters to the editor (and the police). Jack's contemporaries contributed much to the night-marish story he inscribed with his knife on the bodies of his victims.

Murder News as Cultural Event

If murder is a social (as well as antisocial) act, then its telling and selling by the press are significant cultural events that reveal much about what journalists think the public wants or needs to know. Murder news by definition both whets and feeds an appetite that disapproving critics deem perverse or voyeuristic. Why, we may well ask, are so many of us drawn to images of violence that frighten or disgust us? What is the source of our ambivalent response to scenes or images of horror in films, on television, and in newspapers? (Why do we slow down and stare at a car crash while driving along the highway when we have no intention of helping any of the victims?) Some tentative answers to these questions lie scattered through the following pages. For the present we need but allude to [Women's Studies Scholar] Cynthia Freeland's observation that pornography and the horror film share in common not only multiple participants and body parts, but also "the *embodiment* of humans" or "intimacies of the flesh." Murder news, then, is not just about extreme violence inflicted on someone else. As [author Richard] Tithecott points out, it is also about our own fantasies and the culture out of which they arise. Implicitly or explicitly, feature stories about homicide convey powerful messages about morality, respectability, and normality. For example, the Victorian press often garnished murder news with allusions to the wages of sin, which had the effect of moving readers to imagine themselves as either victim or victimizer, thereby giving rise to the thought "There but for the grace of God go I."

Crime news is, of course, only one form of storytelling. Because most of us have been immersed in stories of one kind or another since childhood, we find it hard to resist narratives and narrativizing. Some years ago Joan Didion addressed our collective hunger for stories that contain a moral, especially those dealing with violent death: "We tell ourselves stories in order to live. . . . We look for the sermon in the suicide, for the social or moral lesson in the murder of five. We interpret what we see, select the most workable of the multiple choices. We live entirely, especially if we are writers, by the imposition of a narrative, line upon disparate images, by the 'ideas' with which we have learned to freeze the shifting phantasmagoria which is our actual experience."

Narrative as Coping Mechanism

This notion of freezing the ever-slurring phantasms of our own lived experience conjures up another vital aspect of murder stories—namely, the ways in which the narrative form helps us to cope with the fears that well up inside us whenever we encounter scenes of terror or sites of horror. As Wes Craven, the director of the notorious *Scream* films, observed, "It's like boot camp for the psyche. In real life human beings are packaged in the flimsiest of packages, threatened by real and sometimes horrifying dangers, events like Columbine. But the narrative form puts those fears into a manageable series of events. It gives us a way of thinking rationally about our fears." Craven then went on to reveal how much he enjoyed the search for ways to heighten the fears of his audience:

"They see patterns, and they try to think logically about how to escape the lurking danger. Our job is to always stay one or two steps ahead and keep them scared."

Because the Whitechapel killer was never caught and put on trial, the murders became the kind of mystery that resisted simple, let alone seamless, emplotment. Detective fiction buffs need no reminding of the pleasure of the denouement, when the master sleuth (more often nowadays the medical examiner or forensic pathologist) unmasks the villain and thereby helps to restore order and heal the gaping wound in the community. The Ripper's elusiveness denied both the police and the public the kind of closure that comes with the arrest, conviction, and (in Victorian England) execution of the murderer. Instead of a reassuring end to the story, these mutilation murders left gaps into which all kinds of theories, daydreams, and nightmares rushed pell-mell. Bereft of an explanation, contemporaries also had good reason to fear that the perpetrator would soon strike again so long as he remained free. Thus the silences in our newspaper texts problematize the narrative and create countless breaks or ruptures that invite more speculation. When dealing with the Ripper reportage, then, one would do well to bear in mind the warning phrase still heard every day in the London underground [subway]: *Mind the gap.*

Media Motives

Beyond our love of stories lies the attraction or news about sex and violence involving people other than ourselves and our families and friends. Such news usually sends shudders of horror or frissons down our spines, and may well inspire a fleeting sense of schadenfreude [taking joy in the pain of others]. Sometimes we justify our fondness for the gory details by intellectualizing them. In the words of Psychiatrist Theodore Dalrymple: "Murderers and their deeds raise acutely the fundamental moral and psychological questions of our existence, which is why there are so many murders in literature. The proper study of mankind is murder." In any event, the priority given by the media to murder news reveals much about the anxieties of any culture and society, and this applies with special force to the Ripper reportage. As [German Literature professor] Maria Tatar has shrewdly observed about another time and culture (Weimar Germany), "the representation of murdered women must function as an aesthetic strategy for managing certain kinds of sexual, social, and political anxieties and for constituting an artistic and social identity." Seen in this light, murder news is not only heavily laden with gentler conflicts and social inequities, it also reveals how the media package such reports with an eye to either raising or allaying the fears of readers, and to enhancing the appeal of the next day's edition.

Stories of real murder continue to fascinate, especially if they deal with bizarre perpetrators and unusual modes of killing. Harold Schechter, a professor of American literature and culture in New York City, has raised the narration of homicidal acts to an art form in a book that dwells in the twilight zone between the fictional and the factual. In *Fiend: The Shocking True Story of America's Youngest Serial Killer* (2000), he recounts with some of the novelistic skills of Caleb Carr the sadistic crime spree of Jesse Harding Pomeroy, a deeply disturbed youth from South Boston who between 1872 and 1874 tortured and sexually molested over a dozen small boys before stabbing to death and severely mutilating a four-year-old boy. For this latter murder the perverse Pomeroy earned the enduring epithet "the Boy Fiend," and spent more than fifty years in prison.

Murder News in Victorian Society

Although written more than thirty years ago, Richard D. Altick's *Victorian Studies in Scarlet* (1970) remains the best starting point for any inquiry into the import of murder news in Victorian England. Drawing on the trial transcripts compiled by such murder buffs as Henry B. Irving and William Roughead. Altick ranged over some fifteen high-profile murders between 1849 and 1903. However, his blithe assumption that the public's passionate interest in such cases helped to "ease the social tensions of the time" seems rather wide of the mark. By featuring certain homicides and by employing reporters who specialized in murder, the London press had by midcentury succeeded in taking this subgenre of news out of the hands of publishers of ha'penny broadsides or street cocks and had begun to captivate a huge audience—young and old, male and female alike—by means of blood-curdling stories of violence and mystery. Altick's final chapter, "Murder and the Victorian Mind," begins with a rhetorical question: "Who can account for the prevalence of murder in Victorian England?" However, one remarkable feature of Victorian society was the relative infrequency of murder, considering the hordes of pauperized people crowded together in dirty and fetid tenements, the extent of class antagonism, and the amount of alcohol consumed. While the population of England and Wales rose from roughly twenty to twenty-nine million between 1861 and 1891, the annual number of recorded homicides between 1857 and 1890 averaged only 369. Rarest of all murders were those committed by middle and upper-class perpetrators, especially women or ladies, even though females were more likely to be indicted for murder than for any other felony. The banality of most murders in England meant that newspaper editors were constantly on the lookout for "good" or unusual homicides that would grab and hold the attention of readers for days or weeks on end.

Following in Altick's wake, various Victorianists have cultivated the fertile field of murder, ranging from the single crime of passion to serial killings. English professor Thomas Boyle's engagingly subjective tour of sensational crimes in the mid-Victorian period draws heavily on the press clippings of an English naval surgeon obsessed by such morbid fare. The literary critic John Cawelti has speculated about the ways murder news affected Victorian readers, who were supposedly filled with feelings of guilt, anger, and sexual desire. Needless to say, cases of domestic murder, involving family members, friends, lovers, or servants, held a special fascination for respectable Victorians, who were well aware of the emotions or desires that might drive someone to commit the ultimate crime. Few of these studies, however—with the notable exception of Altick's *Deadly Encounters* (1986)—directly address the reporting of murder in the press, though at least one late-Victorian crime aficionado, Dr. John Watson, knew just how widely the accounts of any given crime varied from one newspaper to another.

Coverage Criteria

The history of murder news raises many questions about the criteria used by editors to decide which crimes deserved special attention. Why, we may well ask, were some homicides assigned feature status while others were relegated to mere filler at the bottom of the page? Alas, we know so little about the inner workings of the Victorian press, especially the reasons behind the editorial decisions made every day about the content and layout of every newspaper. (As a youthful copyboy working for the *New York Times*, I often wondered what went on when the senior editors or newsroom moguls gathered together in the "bullpen" at night to discuss the next day's paper.) Apart from the anecdotal memoirs of the leading lights of Fleet Street, who relished tales of their more eccentric colleagues, all we have in the way of evidence are the printed results of the editorial decisions taken; and unlike today, we have to contend with anonymity in the Victorian era, when most journalists never knew the joy of a byline. While one murder trial might earn three full columns, another would merit only a short paragraph. That seasoned connoisseur of murder trials William Roughead once declared, "We have in

Scotland a really good murder about once in five years," while England, "more favoured in matters criminal, boasts one a week." Chief among his criteria of a "good" homicide were "striking circumstances, the picturesque, unusual setting, and the curious character of the chief actors."

Such criteria help to explain why Fleet Street made such a splash out of the ten-day trial of Alfred John Monson in the High Court of Justiciary, Edinburgh, in December 1893. A moneylender and opportunist, Monson was accused of murdering his well-born pupil Lieutenant Windsor Dudley Cecil Hambrough, aged twenty, while shooting rabbits at Ardlamont House near the Kyles of Bute in Argyleshire. Monson told the police that Hambrough's gun had discharged while he was climbing over a wall. But there was conflicting evidence about the gun that fired the fatal shot, and Monson turned out to be the beneficiary of a large insurance policy in the event of Hambrough's death. At first the London papers ran only a few short articles about the shooting. But their response to Monson's trial was overwhelming. More than a hundred pressmen from all over the country covered the proceedings— including seventy reporters, twenty-one "descriptive writers," and fifteen artists. The *Times* alone ran a total of twenty columns on the trial, consisting mostly of the paraphrased testimony of witnesses. Dismissing the prosecution's argument that Monson was a consummate liar, the jury returned a verdict of "not proven," and the defendant left the courthouse to cheers from the crowd waiting outside.

Sensationalism

The media hype surrounding this case says a good deal about the nature of journalistic sensationalism. What exactly was it about this case that drew so many reporters as well as spectators to the trial? Was it the elitist ambience of the shooting party, the victim's Oxonian ties, or Monson's financial intrigues? Here was a murder laden with mystery and scented with snobbery. How very different was the media's response to the trial in 1889—also in Edinburgh—of a plebeian baby farmer named Jessie King, who had strangled three illegitimate infants whom she had adopted for a cash advance. While the trial attracted many spectators, the *Times* awarded it only twenty-three lines of small print. In almost every respect the contrast between these two stories could not have been greater. Clearly Fleet Street regarded infanticide in a Scottish slum, without any element of mystery and devoid of elitism, as undeserving of feature status.

Fascination with murder was not confined to newspapers. Witness all the shilling shockers, penny dreadfuls, ha'penny broadsides, penny gaffs, and melodramas about unnatural death in plebeian settings. The crowded galleries in courtrooms during highly publicized murder trials also attest to the drawing power of this crime. For all the curious people— many of them women—who could not get into the courtroom, the press provided the only access to the case. When it came to bloodshed, Victorian readers seemed to relish the details of what knives, axes, bullets, or other lethal weapons had done to the victims' bodies. Many of the morbid details revealed in the press would be deemed unfit to print today even in the most Murdochian tabloids. Descriptions of bodies stabbed, shot, poisoned, and dismembered—what I call sensation-horror news—composed the centerpieces of feature stories about the inquests and trials in homicide cases. Thus a good deal of Victorian murder news qualifies as "gorenography" because the clinical or anatomical details published offered a fine feast for the eyes of more prurient readers. . . .

Issues Underlying Reports

. . . In sum, the press coverage of the Whitechapel murders reveals much about late Victorian culture, or what cultural critic Raymond Williams called "structures of feeling" and "the *informing spirit* of a whole way of life." Like other kinds of news, the reporting of murder involves "the structures of meaning based on historical constructs," while reflecting the ideological and material interests of the newspaper industry at large. Murder news also reinforces the codes of normative or respectable behavior that are supposed to protect the integrity of the family—indeed, the whole social order. Since murder represents the ultimate social and moral transgression, readers of these stories yearned for reassurance that the criminal justice system worked and that the villain would pay dearly for his wickedness. In an increasingly secular age, editors or leader (editorial) writers took on the clergy's traditional task of preaching about the wages of sin and the necessity of avoiding temptation. Not just keen to sell more papers, they also wished to remind readers about the terrible fate that awaited anyone who succumbed to the desires that had ended in this particular tragedy or scandal. After all, one did not have to be a "born criminal" to progress (or regress) rapidly from venial to mortal sin and thence to prison or the scaffold. Murder news thus reflected the Victorian obsession with character and virtuous conduct. No matter how much the Whitechapel murders differed from the standard fare of domestic murder, the fundamental issues of morality and depravity also underlay the reporting of these horrors.

Movies Have a Wide Range of Influence on Youth

W. W. Charters

This excerpt is from a summary by W. W. Charters on scientific research performed in the 1930s called the Payne Fund studies. These studies represent the first organized, comprehensive effort to examine the social effects of the mass media. Movies, the form of mass media under scrutiny, were increasingly popular in that era due to the addition of sound to film.

Charters' piece explains some of the research results: what kind of information children retain upon watching movies, to what extent children recall what they have seen in the movies, and whether children can distinguish between reality and fiction in movies. Charters also notes that children experience movies differently and more intensely than adults. In his view, movies have a powerful influence—good and bad—over the education and guidance of children.

W. W. Charters was Professor and Director of the Bureau of Educational Research at Ohio State University until his death in 1952. He was also the Chairman of the Payne Fund studies.

How much information children acquire from the movies is a question of interest to parents and is a matter of concern to them when their children view pictures which the parents do not like. In the latter case, the problem is accompanied by fear if the parent believes that his children learn much from the picture and is dismissed lightly if he thinks that most of what they see passes over their heads.

What Children Retain

To the question of how much children retain of what is in a picture for them to see, Holaday and Stoddard directed their

W.W. Charters, "Learning Facts," *Motion Pictures and Youth: A Summary*. New York: The Macmillan Company, 1933, pp. 7–11, 39–42.

attention in a three-year study. They used seventeen commercial pictures such as "Tom Sawyer," "New Moon," "Stolen Heaven," "Rango," "Passion Flower," and "Fighting Caravans." Somewhat over 3,000 children and adults participated in the study as observers. They were selected in four age groups which were all given the same tests upon the information acquired. These tests were of two types, one testing the retention of the plot of the story—the actions and sayings of the actors,—the other testing the general information of historical, geographical, or mechanical items. To the 3,000 individuals were administered a total of 26 tests each containing from 30 to 64 factual items and producing an aggregate of more than 20,000 testings for a total of 813,000 items attempted. Proper precautions were taken to equate groups for age, intelligence, and the like so that the results from group to group might be comparable. Careful statistical techniques were utilized.

The most striking conclusion translated roughly into concrete language is this. If parents take their 8 year old child to the movies he will catch three out of every five items that the parents catch. This conclusion is arrived at somewhat as follows. The next day after viewing each of six pictures in 1930 to 1931 and answering a total of approximately 400 carefully selected questions dealing with items appearing in the scenes, 162 "superior" adults—young college professors, graduate students and their wives—made a score of 87.8 out of a possible 100. At the same time 959 children in grades 2 and 3 made a score of 52.5. Coincidentally 1,180 children in grades 5 and 6 made a score of 65.9 and youths in grades 9 and 10 achieved a score of 80.9. Thus using the adult score as a basis, children of 8 and 9 years made 60 per cent, those of 11 and 12 made 75 per cent, and children of 15 and 16 made 91 per cent of the score obtained by adults. Hence roughly speaking a parent who is a superior adult can count upon his young child to see approximately 3 out of the 5 things he sees, his 11 or 12 year old child to see 3 out of 4, and his 15 or 16 year old to catch

9 out of 10. Or putting the conclusion in another way the 8 or 9 year old sees half of what is to be seen, the 11 or 12 year old two thirds, and the 15 or 16 year old four fifths of what is to be seen. This is true if we assume, as a reading of the study demonstrates, that the questions in the tests are a reasonably fair sample of the questions that might be asked. The amount of information acquired is very high.

What Children Recall

A second interesting fact relates to the surprising amount the children remember about a picture six weeks and three months later. In general the second-third-grade children at the end of six weeks remember 90 per cent of what they knew on the day following the show. Three months after seeing the picture they remember as much as they did six weeks after seeing it. In some cases, as with "Tom Sawyer," they remember more at the end of six weeks and still more at the end of three months. At all ages including the adults the slow drop of the curve of forgetting is striking. The investigators conclude from the data that the "curves of retention are considerably higher than those obtained by previous investigators (using other materials) and motion pictures appear to make a greater contribution to visual education than was previously suspected."

Of interest is an implication lying within the fact that very young children remember correctly 50 or 60 per cent of what they see. Conversely this means that they do not get 50 or 40 per cent of what they see. When they do not answer questions accurately it may not mean that their memories are blank on those points. They may have acquired misinformation. Dysinger and Ruckmick found in their interviews that children frequently misunderstood the meaning of what they had seen and thereby reacted in unexpected fashion at their "reading points."

Movies as Reality

A third interesting fact of educational significance drawn from the study is this. Children of all ages tend to accept as authentic what they see in the movies. Thus pre-tests on general information were given to groups and their scores were computed. Then equated groups viewed pictures in which were shown the errors of fact which had been covered in the pretests. The two sets of scores were compared and it was found that at each of the three age levels the incorrectly shown items had left their marks. The children had increased their fund of knowledge on the correctly shown items covered by the test, but their acceptance of the incorrect items as correct had lowered their improvement in their total scores. They tended to accept the errors as facts. In general "children accept the information in the movies as correct unless it is flagrantly incorrect."

It is of interest to know the types of fact that children remember best. The investigators divided the facts into ten classes and found that "action was remembered best when it concerned sports, general conversation, crime, and fighting, when it had a high emotional tonus and when it occurred in a familiar type of surrounding such as home, school, or tenement. . . . It was understood least when it concerned unfamiliar activities such as bootlegging and business, when it had practically no emotional tonus, and when it occurred in surroundings of an unfamiliar and interesting type such as café and frontier."

Information Observed

The types of information tested in this study are supplemented by the Blumer and Thrasher studies. They analyze the rôle of the movies as a source of information which is noticed and copied by adolescents. In their studies they mass cases covering a wide variety of areas in which information is acquired and used: hints on how to beautify one's self and wear one's clothes, examples of attractive mannerisms, and demonstrations of satisfying love techniques. To these they add patterns for the play of children, suggestions for delinquent action and crime upon occasion. None of these was measured by Blumer and Thrasher with the Holaday-Stoddard techniques, but it may reasonably be assumed that the acquisition of facts in these specific areas described by Blumer and Thrasher proceeds with the same effectiveness as in the areas studied by Holaday and Stoddard.

Finally no significant sex differences appeared in the amount of information acquired or the amount remembered at later dates. Girls and boys remember about equally well.

In summary Holaday and Stoddard have shown that the amount of information gained from motion pictures by children of all ages including the 8 and 9 year olds is "tremendously high." This constitutes the first link in the sequential chain of the inquiry into the influence of motion pictures upon children and youth. . . .

Emotional Possession

The intensity of child experience in viewing pictures cannot be fully appreciated by adults. To adults the picture is good or bad, the acting satisfactory or unsatisfactory, the singing up to or not up to standard. To them a picture is just a picture. They may recall memories of thrills they used to have but the memories are pale in comparison to the actual experience. They get a more vivid impression of this excitement by watching a theater full of children as a thrilling drama unreels. They see the symptoms of keen emotion. But even in the presence of these manifestations they miss the depth and intensity of the child's experience.

Several factors contribute to emotional possession. The actions and the setting are concrete. When in the fairy story the child is told that the prince led his troops into battle he has to provide his own imagery; but in the picture he sees the charming prince at the head of a band of "real" men. Every significant visual image is provided before his eyes in the motion picture. He does not have to translate the words in which the story is conveyed. He sees machines; he does not hear about them. He visits the islands of the southern seas in a real ship; he does not have to listen to a narrator describe the scenes in words alone. The motion picture tells a very concrete and simple tale in a fashion which makes the story easy to grasp.

Emotional possession is also caused by the dramatic forms of the picture. One of the objectives of drama is to arouse the emotions. Indeed, the weakness of many "teaching films" is the absence of dramatic elements—often necessarily omitted because of the nature of the content to be taught. But in the commercial movies and in teaching films of action, the dramatic flow of the story stirs the emotions and produces that intensity of experience which Blumer calls "emotional possession."

A third factor which contributes its influence to this condition is the attractiveness of the pictures—beautiful and thrilling scenes, interesting people, attractive persons moving on the stage, stimulating colors, expert lighting, and the like. The child wants to be a part of such a bit of life. He does not pull back from the experience; he hurls himself into it.

Movies as an Education Medium

All of these factors and probably others produce a condition that is favorable to certain types of learning. This is the quality of authority. Children accept as true, correct, proper, right what they see on the screen. They have little knowledge. The people on the screen are confidence-producing. Everything works to build up a magnificent and impressive world. Holaday and Stoddard found the children accepting both fact and error as fact. Blumer indicates the power of movie patterns upon conduct. The authority of the screen may account for some of the striking change of attitude of children found by Peterson and Thurstone.

All of these considerations lead inevitably to the increasing strength of the conclusion that the motion picture is an extremely powerful medium of education.

A second conclusion drawn from the report is that the range of influence of movies is very wide. Blumer found in studying two thousand children what every parent knows about his own child—that the movies dominate the patterns of play of children in a wide variety of forms. He presents scores of cases to show that the world of phantasy of young children and adolescents and of both sexes is ruled by movie subjects. Dozens of cases are presented to show the effects of the movies in stimulating emotions of fright, sorrow, love, and "excitement." Cases are presented to illustrate how the movies give children techniques of action in situations which are of interest to them ranging from the trivial techniques of the playground to disturbing cues for the delinquent. And most far-reaching of all he indicates how they stir powerful ambitions, good and bad; develop permanent ideals, high and low; and crystallize the framework of life careers. In most unexpected quarters the influence of the movies is discovered in the reports of Blumer and Thrasher and their associates.

A third concept which supplements emotional possession and range of influence is the guidance concept which grows out of the preceding paragraph. Children are born into a world of which they know nothing. They are little individualists who have laboriously to learn how to fit into social groups. They possess impulses, instincts, wishes, desires, which drive them on to seek experience, adventure, and satisfaction. They are avidly interested in everything that seems to them to be able to provide what they want.

The Power of Motion Pictures

Yet they know so little and are so anxious to learn. They seek information, stimulation, and guidance in every direction. They are often confused, frequently maladjusted, and sometimes without confidence. In this situation the motion picture seems to be a godsend to them. While they are being entertained they are being shown in attractive and authoritative fashion what to do. They are guided in one direction or another as they absorb rightly or wrongly this idea or that one. Sometimes the guidance is good, at other times it is bad. Sometimes it lies in a direction opposed to the teachings of the home or the school; at other times it reinforces them. But always the motion picture is potentially a powerfully influential director. Not the only guide which leads them, to be sure: the community, chums and playmates, the home, the school, the church, the newspapers, all are used by these omnivorous seekers after the kinds of experience they want. But among them the motion picture possesses potency so substantial that society must not fail to understand and see that it is used beneficently in the guidance of children.

Mass Media Is Teaching Violence as a Solution to Problems

Fredric Wertham

In the following viewpoint Fredric Wertham argues that mass media provides the public with an alternative "education" by teaching that violence is a solution to problems. The author was among the first to identify the social consequences of violence in the media. At the time of Wertham's research in the 1960s, mass media was comprised of radio, films, television, magazines, and comic books.

According to Wertham, "mass media" and "violence" are inextricably linked terms. He maintains that the mass media became a school for violence for two reasons. First, technological advances expanded the kinds of media developed as well as the distribution and accessibility of those media. Secondly, for many years there was a societal oversight concerning the effects of violence in the media—particularly its effects on children. Wertham investigates the reasons for violence in the media as well as the arguments that are invoked to defend such portrayals of violence. In his view, denying the effects of violence in the media is an evasion of truth. He concludes that mass media does not just contribute to a social problem but that it is *a social problem.*

Wertham was a psychiatrist whose research focused on the harmful psychological effects of violence in the media on children. He was the author of three books and numerous articles on the subject. His critique on the comic book industry led to a U.S. Congressional inquiry and the subsequent creation of the regulatory Comics Code.

Fredric Wertham, *A Sign for Cain: An Exploration of Human Violence*. New York: Scribner, 1966, pp. 193–196, 216–217, 221, 226–228. Copyright © 1966 by Fredric Wertham. All rights reserved. Reprinted with the permission of Scribner, an imprint of Simon & Schuster Adult Publishing Group.

To discuss violence without referring to mass media is as impossible as to discuss modern mass media without referring to violence. If somebody had said a generation ago that a school to teach the art and uses of violence would be established, no one would have believed him. He would have been told that those whose mandate is the mental welfare of children, the parents and the professionals, would prevent it. And yet this education for violence is precisely what has happened and is still happening: we teach violence to young people to an extent that has never been known before in history.

Education for Violence

This has become possible through two circumstances. One, of course, consists in tremendous technological advances. The other is the fact that the effects of mass media on the young were not sufficiently recognized. It was a new dimension of the environmental influence on the child. That some ingredients might do and have done harm was as little suspected as it was with cigarette smoking until it was studied clinically.

Solution by violence is a great temptation; control of violence is a difficult task. That is why promotion of violence in all its forms and disguises is a threat to progress. For thousands of years mankind has striven to get away from it. All the wise men who have ever written and spoken about it . . . have said more or less the same thing. But what happens is that we, at the height of power and prosperity, fill the minds of children with an endless stream of images of violence, often glamorous, always exciting. The youngest children are stimulated and encouraged to a primitive response of "hitting out." That, in the School for Violence, is the elementary lesson. Preschool children learn it. The TV program *The Three Stooges* is an ideal primer. The advanced course is the pursuit of happiness by violence.

That there is an inordinate amount of violence in the mass media is an indisputable fact. No other ingredient plays such a predominant role. If one wanted to list all possible varieties and methods of killing, torturing, or injuring people, no more complete source would be available than the modern mass media. Textbooks of forensic psychiatry and criminology are left far behind.

Violence in Comic Books

The modern child is exposed to a variety of mass media: radio, movies, television, comic books, magazines. Even bubble-gum cards (often ugly and violent) may be included. These media have fundamental differences in their manner of technical production and their distribution. They also have socially and aesthetically different values. So for most problems, each would have to be taken up separately. But as far as violence content and its effect are concerned, they may be considered together. At different ages and in varying degrees, many children, or the peer group with which they are in contact, may be exposed to all of them. There is also considerable overlapping, as when more and more movies are shown on television. A nonvisual medium like radio, although by no means violence-free, has least effect. Crime comic books are at the bottom, with very little aesthetic value and great impact on the youngest child. They have demonstrably influenced not only the taste of children but—being so successful in their formulas—also the television producers.

Comic books are the greatest publishing success in history. They were made possible by a special printing process. One edition is about 500,000 copies. (Comic books are to be distinguished from newspaper comic strips, which are very different. The comic-book industry encourages confusion of the two.) Millions of comic books are published every month. At one time, 100,000,000 comic books were published a month (not a year, but a *month*). No other publishing undertaking has ever approached this number. The vast majority of these comic books were not funny and animal comics (which adults assumed they were) but were *crime* comic books; that is to say, they dealt with crime and violence. Their settings may vary, but the substance is the same, whether depicted in the jungle, in the home, on the street, in an urban environment, in a Western setting, on the sea, in outer space, or wherever. Many war comics belong to the same category, with the crime and violence dressed up in patriotic disguise.

The wildest scenes are now not being published any more, although violence still abounds. But the older comic books are still around in large numbers—and in the hands of children—being sold and traded.

Killing in Comics

Killing is commonplace. In one story (not a whole comic book, but one story in it) there are, for example, thirty-seven killings. Brutality, torture, and sadism are featured. The connection between cruelty and sex is stressed in millions of comic books. Girls are flagellated even in a Western setting. Or in an Oriental setting the mysterious villain threatens the half-nude heroine: "I know that you shall love me and be loyal after you have taken a dozen or so lashes across your beautiful back." Just after she has undressed for bed, the "debutante of the year" is stabbed so that the blood runs across her breast. The killer is a girl who kills two other girls and plans to kill "half a dozen prominent women." Then, she says, "they'll know I mean business."

Killing is carried out usually by what, in analogy with modern military terminology, one might call conventional means: shooting, stabbing, clubbing, strangling, drowning, burning. The techniques of all these methods are very fully described. But unconventional nuclear means are also used. For example, radioactive dust is squirted on the markedly protruding breast of a gift. Special varieties of hurting and killing are often shown. One of these is deliberate injury to the eyes. This is so frequent and has induced so many children to try it out that my associates and I have classified it as the "eye motif."

Shooting policemen to the accompaniment of contemptuous remarks belongs to the comic-book repertory. The police officer asks the driver for his license. "It's a pleasure," says the driver, and shoots him: *Bang!* It seems strange that shooting a policeman is considered an especially serious crime and at the same time an especially suitable entertainment for children. The public was astonished when in recent race riots, youngsters attacked the police. We have been teaching them for years that is the thing to do. It is part of the advanced course. . .

Reasons for Violence in the Media

Violent acts, both mild and serious, may be the result of very different psychological processes. In an equally great variety of ways, the mass-media factor may be connected with these processes. At one extreme it may merely tip the scales at the last moment. Only a slight impetus may be needed to translate ideas into actions. At the other extreme it may be a prime incitement and incentive.

Usually the effect lies between: crime and violence shows arouse an appetite for violence, reinforce it when it is present, show a method to carry it out, teach the best way to get away with it, stimulate the connection between cruelty and sex (sadism), blur the child's awareness of its wrongness. That is the curriculum of the School for Violence.

Why *is* there so much violence in the mass media? That is a question not to be shirked. Is it merely accidental? Can we dismiss it as merely a symptom of the times?

There are three main reasons. First, violence is exciting. It is an effective attention-getting device. You know the story of the man who said he could persuade a mule to do anything—by first whacking him over the head to get his attention. We have become somewhat like that mule. Violence onstage is an easy way to arouse interest, win an audience, and hold it. To keep the interest up, more and more violence is needed. In the words of a film critic, the appeal of violence "is calculated as coldly as if it were money—which indeed it is."

Second, mass-media violence is a reflection of a part of our social reality. There are people who half-consciously believe that violence is a good method for solving problems. They may not intend it explicitly in the individual case, but they tolerate it because they think the violent are the strong and will win. The imagination of some statesmen does not seem to reach much further. They want to send the marines as quickly as Superman flies out the window.

Third, the excessive display of violence exists against the back-ground of a whole system of defense arguments, alibis, and rationalizations. The same or very similar reasons are repeated over and over again with the resounding voice of conviction. One or the other continually crops up in newspapers, magazines, books or scientific papers, publicity releases, radio and TV discussions, PTA meetings, practically all the books on mass-media effects, government brochures, articles about juvenile delinquency, mental-hygiene pamphlets, and so on.

Some Claims

What makes these arguments and others like them so important is that they not only amount to an acceptance of violence in advance, but are applied also to other social evils, such as poverty, slums, racism, alcoholism, and so on. They are comforting assumptions and evasions which tend to relieve us of responsibility. It is necessary to take a good look at them.

It is variously claimed:

That the emotionally healthy and well-adjusted child from a harmonious family is not harmed—as if we could be sure of such a blanket immunity against the suggestive and seductive influences to which millions of children are exposed. The healthiest child from the most harmonious family may have some weak points that are not readily apparent. Every normal child is immature and therefore susceptible to harmful influences.

That it is all up to the family to shield the child—as if we were still living on farms and in the preelectronic age. It is fashionable to blame parents, especially mothers, for any kind of maladjustment of their offspring. In this way, all the outside influences are disregarded—those which come to the child over the parents' heads and over, which the family has little control. Parents have been so brainwashed into a belief in their own guilt that it is hard to reverse it. John Ruskin wrote long ago: "If good fathers and mothers always had as good children, the world would soon be angelic." To put all the emphasis on the family means to bypass the community, the society which conditions the family....

...*That critique of mass-media violence may lead to censorship and interfere with civil liberties.* Social control for the protection of children has nothing to do with censorship for adults. Children have the right to grow up healthy and uncorrupted. The battle for civil liberties should not be fought on the backs of children. Those who fight for freedom of expression would be in a stronger position if they conceded that outspoken sadism should be withheld from children.

The argument that control of what is advertised and exposed to children would interfere with civil liberties has no historical foundation. Civil liberties are not guaranteed but are vilified if under their protection children are harmed. It has never happened in the history of the world that regulations to protect children—be they with regard to child labor, food, drink, arms, sex, publications, entertainment, or plastic toys—have played any role whatsoever in the abridgment of political or civil liberties for adults. Where freedom has fallen, it has come about in totally different ways....

Evasive Terms

That mass media cannot really cause *any harm, but merely trigger it.* The word "triggering" as a substitute for "causing" is fashionable but loaded. It is as if a man who shot somebody to death would say, "I did not cause his death, I merely pulled the trigger." In mental life there is no mechanical, automatic causation. Stimuli that set things in motion or reinforce them or continue them merge with one another.

A similarly evasive and even more fashionable term is "basic." It comes in many versions and is used in every conceivable context. Mass media cannot touch the "basic personality structure"; they cannot be a "basic cause" or a "basic traumatic factor"; they cannot influence "basic processes" or "basic reactions"; the "basically normal child" is not affected; whatever causes trouble is "deeper and more basic." Such a term as "basic" in this connection is purely subjective and pretentious. It means whatever a writer wishes it to mean. This is not where science can begin, but where it ends. Eighty percent of the mortality in the United States is accounted for by three conditions: cardiovascular diseases, cancer, accidents. In none of them do we know the "basic" cause, but in all of them we know a great deal about contributing and conditioning factors. It is this knowledge which enables us to treat and prevent. In the same way, in medical psychology, attention must be paid not only to the search for "basic" causes, which in human behavior are elusive anyhow, but to any conditioning and contributing factors—physical, psychological, and environmental-social.

Another glibly applied term is "aggression." It is often used as an innocuous-sounding substitute for "violence." It is also used to mean a cause of violence—or again something different from violence. Freud regarded "aggression" originally as sadism, that is, as a part of sexuality. Later he used it interchangeably with "destruction." Currently, "aggression" is a fashionable term applied in an ambiguous way to mean something constructive or destructive or neutral. Frequently it includes—and conceals—the intent and fact of naked violence. Abstract discussions of aggression have little value. Any big psychological generalization with the term "aggression" is apt not to explain but to becloud the issue.

Factors and Influences

That only contact with significant real persons in the child's life influences him, while pictures and printed words do not. The great success of the many printed advertisements and television commercials directed at children would indicate that they have considerable effect. This is well known to the "significant real persons" who have to pay for the advertised products.

That when children say that they saw something in the mass media, they are making it up just as an excuse. This implies complete misunderstanding of the clinical examination. The careful clinician does not suggest anything to a child by leading questions, nor does he accept anything at its face value. Among the many children examined by my associates and myself, what's more, no child has ever volunteered the statement about mass media as an excuse for anything he had done. Typical is the case of a seven-year-old boy who set fires. He said nothing about either comic books or television, but when asked what he saw on a Rorschach plate during a test, he began a long stream of talk about monsters who cause explosions and set fires.

That so many factors enter into a child's development that we cannot gauge the effect of any single one. This would mean that scientific study of human behavior is not possible and that the status quo is inscrutable.

The only-one-factor argument comes sometimes in the form of "Mass media violence is only one little thing" in a child's life. The answer is that it is just many "little things" which determine a child's development.

That children are not affected by mass-media violence because they know that it is only make-believe and not really true. Suppose you showed on television a bed and a man and a woman doing something they should not be doing on TV. Would you let your small child watch that and say, "Oh, she knows that is just make-believe"? In sex we realize this is suggestive and exciting. But when it comes to violence, we are blinded.

Quite apart from the fact that it is not always easy for children to distinguish between what is fantasy and what reality, this argument comes from a misunderstanding of how propaganda works, for children as well as adults. Propaganda is based not on reason and truth but on emotion. . . .

Media as Social Problem

. . . That the character of a child has "jelled" at the age of seven (others say at five or three) and that later influences are therefore negligible. This, like some of the other arguments, is misunderstood and misapplied Freud. As Alexander Pope wrote: "So by false learning is good sense defaced." Of course, early infantile experiences play a role. But they do not determine the future course of a person mechanically and fatalistically. To say, as often has been said, that mass media cannot do harm unless the parent-child relationships had been disturbed in the first place is unscientific both for practical purposes and in theory. What Freud said about outside influences was that up to the age of sixteen or seventeen, children were "still in the formative period . . . and ought not to be exposed to perverse influences." And in one of his last writings, he stated about the causes of disturbed behavior that in addition to early childhood experiences, "we must not forget to include the influence of civilization."

That to see a relationship between mass media and behavior means using mass media as a scapegoat for social problems. The modern mass media in their present state *are* a social problem.

CHAPTER 2

Media Violence Issues from the 1960s to the 1980s

Chapter Preface

By the 1960s, films were a veteran of the entertainment industry and television was well-established. The growth of the entertainment industry, coupled with building-block research on media violence (mostly on children) and burgeoning cultural interest in social issues, led to more widely spread interest in the debate.

Violence in visual media was not limited to entertainment. Television news broadcasts also began to show increasingly graphic imagery—called "reality violence" by some scholars—of current events such as the Vietnam War. This was the first war ever to be covered daily in the news, which explains the nickname "the living room war" bestowed on the conflict. Journalists were "embedded" with American troops and photographed or wrote about their experiences alongside soldiers.

Several still photographs in the news stand out from the period: a 1963 photo of a monk burning himself in protest; a 1968 photo and newsreel footage of a point-blank execution on a Saigon street; and a 1972 image of children suffering from a mistaken napalm strike intended for troops, not civilians.

However, violent images such as this were the exception rather than the rule. Less than one-quarter of the images shown on television reflected death or injury. Conventional wisdom suggests that television "changed" public perception of the war, but polls from the period indicate that opinions started to shift before the Tet Offensive in 1968, a turning point in the war, after which more imagery made its way into news broadcasts. In addition, researchers emphasize that the news was reported with great frequency but that graphic violence comprised relatively little of that reporting. Yet there is no doubt that images that did surface have endured in the public's memory. In essence, coverage of the war may have made a bigger contribution to broadcast precedents than to antiwar protests.

Violent News Images Affect Public Opinion

David Culbert

This article by historian David Culbert analyzes the ramifications of a specific violent image in the media during the Vietnam War. In 1968, a photographer and several newsreel cameramen captured an image of a South Vietnamese colonel performing a point-blank execution on a suspected Vietcong (North Vietnamese) member. The still photograph displays the colonel holding a gun to the other man's temple; the news footage shows the actual execution.

Culbert addresses the consequences of that image: how various members of President Lyndon B. Johnson's administration responded, how the public reacted, and where it is situated in the history of war, propaganda, and film. The author also examines the context of the picture and the debate over whether or not it had an impact on American politics and policy toward the Vietnam War. Culbert concludes that the image is a visual part of the collective American memory about the war and that its overall impact remains a topic of scrutiny.

David Culbert has been professor of history at Louisiana State University since 1971. He is the author of numerous book and articles on the history of film, war, and propaganda.

The Vietnam War is of considerable interest to those who study the impact of visual images on political decision-making, though there is little certitude as to how one incorporates still photographs or television news reports into the process. For example, the 2003 edition of a widely-used college text, *American Public Opinion*, offers this safe conclusion: 'Me-

David Culbert, *War and the Media: Reportage and Propaganda, 1900–2003*. London: I.B. Tauris & Co. Ltd., 2005. Edited by Mark Connelly and David Welch. Copyright © 2005 by Mark Connelly and David Welch. Reproduced by permission.

dia messages can influence opinion in several ways, but the effects are generally modest.' Textbook prose is notorious for avoiding controversy in favor of platitudes, but students of propaganda have every reason to wonder about the oft-noted problem of the so-called 'magic bullet': does a single powerful photograph or television news programme actually have the capacity to alter public attitudes about a particular government policy?. . .

Media and Policy

. . . As a general proposition, the answer is no. Media more often reinforces the decisions of those in power, or trivializes reformation policy by focusing on the irrelevant. Newsreels were notorious for the amount of space given, for example, to bathing beauties. American television news coverage of the Vietnam War for the most part offered little of visual significance, and more often reinforced or followed elite opinion than attacked the status quo, as [Communications Professor] Daniel Hallin has demonstrated persuasively. It is inaccurate to remember America's Vietnam War as a so-called 'living-room war,' in which nightly images of violence turned viewers from hawks to doves. Most shots were taken far from the scene of an actual fire fight, and there are far more instances of helicopters taking of and landing than of close-range fighting.

The beginning of the 1968 Tet Offensive is an important exception. In the fall of 1967 President Lyndon Johnson's popularity began to decline sharply, thanks to the continued unpopular war in Vietnam. Johnson called home the American field commander, General William Westmoreland, and ordered the general to travel around the United States, announcing that American policies were working—that there was, as the phrase of the day put it, 'light at the end of the tunnel.' Westmoreland did as he was told.

The North Vietnamese countered with the most sustained uprising of the entire Vietnam War, the January–April 1968 Tet Offensive, which began on the last day of January 1968, with uprisings which extended into downtown Saigon, the capital of South Vietnam, all-too-close to hotels where foreign television crews stayed. The terrorist arm of North Vietnam, the Vietcong, was brought into the open, in hopes that the populace of South Vietnam would embrace a new North Vietnamese government. The populace did no such thing. The Vietcong was decimated. The North Vietnamese suffered a major military setback. In military terms, the North Vietnamese suffered a severe defeat at the time of the Tet Offensive.

Impact of a Single Photograph

From a psychological point of view, however, the Tet offensive ended up helping the North Vietnamese cause in a profound way. Images of violence in downtown Saigon, including Vietcong terrorists who blew a hole in the wall surrounding the American Ambassador's compound and got into the Ambassador's residence for some hours, made American television viewers—to say nothing of a number of foreign policymakers in Washington, DC—fear that all Vietnam had been overrun by the North Vietnamese. For a time, visual images of disaster numbed Lyndon Johnson into inaction, in spite of what his National Security Advisor, Walt Rostow, insisted to be evidence of a serious North Vietnamese military disaster.

Complicating this difficult situation was a still photograph and television newsfilm taken of a single violent event in downtown Saigon, on 1 February 1968, the execution by Colonel Nguyen Ngoc Loan, head of the South Vietnamese police, of a Vietcong terrorist. The event was captured by two American television news organizations, as well as Associated press photographer Eddie Adams, who won a Pulitzer prize in 1969 for his notorious photograph. The still photograph was shown on the leading nightly American news programme, the

Huntley-Brinkley Report, on the night of 1 February. The next night, 2 February 1968, the color newsfilm of the broadcast was shown to the same large national audience. If one is to make the case for how a single news photograph or visual news story can have an identifiable impact on policy-making, it is with this particular photograph and this particular news story, remembering to take into account the uncertainty so many Americans felt—both elite and non-elite—about what policy American should adopt in terms of supporting or not supporting the Vietnam War.

America became a truly televisual society in the 1960s. America, with a total population of some 202 million, had 78 million television sets. By 1968, television had emerged as the principal source of news for a majority of Americans. Three networks offered nightly thirty-minute news programmes— the American Broadcasting Company (ABC), the Columbia Broadcasting System (CBS), and the National Broadcasting Company (NBC). In 1968 NBC's *Huntley-Brinkley Report,* with commentators Chet Huntley and David Brinkley, was the leading programme, enjoying a nightly audience of some 20 million viewers. CBS's Walter Cronkite [as] slightly behind in the ratings. ABC was a terribly-distant third, in fact so far behind in the ratings as to be little more than a courtesy news source, a situation far removed from what obtains today. It was a day before cable or satellite offered competition. And a day in which no newspaper in American was able to reach a national daily audience, given the vastness of the country and the inability to print the same edition from more than a single east-coast source. *The New York Times* was the paper of record then as now, but the central news source for a national audience was evening news, for thirty minutes, five times a week. Such broadcasts were heavily larded with commercials, so that viewers had at best perhaps eighteen minutes of actual news and news commentary in a typical programme.

Moved by Visual Violence

The Eddie Adams photograph was shown on all three network evening news broadcasts on Thursday, 1 February; the next morning it could be seen on the front pages of newspapers the world over, including both London dailies and British television news programmes. At no other moment in the entire Vietnam War did one event receive such visual reinforcement on television—the Loan photograph on Thursday evening; the colour newsfilm of the same event the following evening. NBC had no idea on 1 February that one of its camera teams had filmed the gruesome event. In fact, NBC had two cameramen covering the event, one with a sound camera, one with a silent one. An American military transport plane flew the footage to Tokyo, where it was developed in a laboratory before being sent by satellite transmission to NBC headquarters in New York City. A cable from Tokyo to New York alerted NBC producer Robert Northshield as to what the footage consisted of. The actual footage was not transmitted to New York until a few minutes before the beginning of the 6:30 EST broadcast on Friday, 2 February.

Some television viewers simply could not believe the violence of the newsfilm, particularly if they saw it in color. Professor Brace Southard, a graduate student in 1968, said he had prepared a modest dinner, consisting of a fried hamburger over which he had poured some catsup. What he was eating suddenly suggested what he was seeing:

> I was just watching the news. General Loan pulled his gun and shot the man, and at first I could not believe that it was happening. It was unlike anything that I had seen before, and then I saw the blood coming out of the guy's head. . . . It really turned my stomach. I didn't throw up but I came close to it. After that I decided what we were doing in Vietnam was wrong. I could not conceive of the callousness with which one person executed another with no pretense,

with no trial, with no evidence. . . . After that I became active in the antiwar movement.

Melodrama Versus Information

Of course not every viewer enjoyed precisely so basic a repast, and not every viewer was moved in the same way with the visual violence. Peter Braestrup, whose two-volume *Big Story* remains the most comprehensive analysis of media coverage of the Tet Offensive, is very uneasy about emotional attempts to read a moral meaning into either the Adams photograph or the NBC newsfilm:

> In journalistic terms, it was fantastic. It is not often that a television cameraman, or a still cameraman for that matter, gets on film happening right there before your eyes one man blowing another man's brains out. . . . It was kind of the supreme melodrama . . . . a kind of super pornography. It evoked strong reactions among those who saw it apparently. . . . It was a kind of ultimate horror story that you captured in living color. But in terms of information it told you almost nothing. That's the chronic problem especially for television and for the still photos, the difference between drama and information.

At one level, Braestrup's statement is unanswerable. What seems to be the execution of one human being by an authority figure may fail to upset some viewers. Indeed, the limitation of all true documentary photographs is precisely the inability to move every viewer in exactly the same way, or even at all. Some undergraduates study the NBC newsfilm in terms of how much gore is presented, and compare its violence with what has been achieved in some recent Hollywood blockbuster. Nor would one want to suggest that a refined aesthetic sensibility was required for images of violence to achieve maximum effect. Professor Southard still has a vivid memory of the Loan rouge; Peter Braestrup was proud to remind his friends that he was a combat veteran of the Korean War, and projected a tough journalist's persona in his later career, a lit cigar at the ready to make everyone know that he was a tough guy.

Impact Not Yet Established

Selected obituaries for Nguyen Ngoc Loan, the police chief who pulled the trigger, remind us that the impact of the photograph and newsfilm has not yet been established. In London, *The Independent*'s Dale Hopper said the Adams photograph 'stunned the world' and 'became a haunting image of the Vietnam War.' The *Washington Post*'s Bart Barnes says the photograph 'stunned millions of leaders' and that the combination of photograph and newsfilm 'contributed to increased popular disillusionment with the war and opposition to the U.S. involvement.' *The New York Times* is of two opinions. Robert McG. Thomas Jr. notes an immediate impact:

> when the film was shown on television and the picture appeared on the front pages of newspapers around the world, the images created an immediate revulsion at a seemingly gratuitous act of savagery that was widely seen as emblematic of a seemingly gratuitous war.

But Thomas then notes that 'for all the emotional impact, the episode had little immediate influence on the tie of American involvement.' *The New York Times*, Richard Bernstein takes a rather different view in a piece published a few months later. There the Adams photograph is captioned: 'This execution is credited with turning public opinion against the war.' He cites with approval the conclusion of Tom Buckley, that the Loan execution was 'the moment when the American public turned against the war.'

A recent *New York Times* public service advertisement about the dangers of drug abuse has a headline which is relevant to the Loan image: 'If you don't want something to be true, does that make it *PROPAGANDA*?' The North Vietnamese felt the photograph was a propaganda success for them during the Tet Offensive. Eddie Adams reports that when he returned to [Saigon] Ho Chi Minh City (as it was then called) in 1983, he was met at the airport by a North Vietnamese journalist who wanted to thank him: 'We have your photograph in the center of our War Museum.'

Photo in Context

What about contextualizing the Loan execution, something not understood by the vast majority of those who saw the film and photograph at the time, to say nothing of those who in retrospect attempt to study the same imagery. We know whom Loan shot, we know that the victim's widow thinks officially, we know where the gun came from, and we know what Loan and Adams think about what they did. Tom Buckley, a *New York Times* reporter who had interviewed Loan in Saigon several times, came to speak with Loan again in 1979, by which time Loan was running a restaurant in a shopping centre south of Washington, DC. Loan's gun, given to him by an American intelligence officer, was a short-barrel .38 Smith & Wesson Airweight. Loan knew personally the man he shot:

> They tell me that he had a revolver, that he wounded one of my policemen, that he spit in the face of the men who captured him. They say that they know this man. He is not a nameless civilian, as the press says. He is Nguyen Tan Dat, alias Han Son. He is the commander of VC sapper unit.

In 1985, NBC's John Hart interviewed the widow of the slain man in Ho Chi Minh City; she dismissed Loan as one of the 'slaves for the imperialists who killed my husband.' Her appearance suggests that she shared her late husband's ideological fanaticism.

In 1979, I spent three hours with Loan at his home in Burke, Virginia, close to his restaurant. Loan offered some additional contextual details, albeit in not quite idiomatic English:

I didn't think about the film—oh the hell with film—next day some American friend say 'what about film'—I had to go to Hue. I have big mouth—sometimes get me into trouble. Accordingly to Southeast Asian philosophy—if you can die it is good—otherwise you have to live. The unit commander of the Vietnamese who should have done it is now in the United States. He called me on phone—he was hesitating—so I did it. We had joint US—Vietnamese teams of MPs. 'You have your responsibility of course'—my wife asked—but why do it?' I did what I shouldn't do. For me I accept the consequences of my act. How about my daughter, day, and night, day and night—my daughter getting married in the near future—how will husband's family respond?

Possible Turning Point

The problem of American television coverage of the Vietnam War has been analysed carefully by Daniel Hallin in his *The 'Uncensored War.'* He reminds readers that what someone remembers is not the same as what happened. He concludes that before February 1968 American television coverage was 'lopsidedly favorable' to Administration policy. He believes that television's 'turnaround' was related to many other changes, a reflection of those changes not an explanation for those changes. He goes yet further: 'there is no way to measure the impact of television's changing images of the war.'

George Herring, author of a widely-used textbook on the Vietnam War, is more insistent: 'A direct link between television reporting and public opinion cannot be established.' Not every scholar agrees. For example, Melvin Small notes that 'Most Americans were shattered by the first television accounts of the 'invasion' of Saigon .... above all, film of the assassination of a suspected Viet Cong infiltrator in cold blood.... Tet was the turning-point in the battle for the hearts and minds of Americans.'

Consider the impact of the violent imagery on some senior aides to Lyndon Johnson. For example White House Counsel Harry McPherson says this about the impact:

> I saw that event on the screen and in the newspapers with two powerful impressions. . . . I knew that the impact of that footage on television and on the American people would be tremendous, that it would hit them very hard, and it gave me all the more a feeling that I should do whatever I could to help us get out as quickly.

Television images of disaster were very much in his mind as he wrote drafts for Johnson's television address on 31 March 1968, the speech where Johnson withdrew from trying to be re-elected as President.

Secretary of State Dean Rusk understood the impact of the Loan footage, shown on the third day of the Tet Offensive. As he watched on Friday night, 2 February, he felt the footage would 'give critics a cause celebre.' Assistant Secretary of State William Bundy also watched that Friday evening. He reportedly felt 'horror and dismay,' claiming it 'cost the government side an 'unnecessary roughing' penalty at a time when it could least afford it.' Congressman Henry S. Reuss of Wisconsin sent an angry letter to General Earle Wheeler, Chairman of the Joint Chiefs of Staff, after seeing the Loan photograph. Nothing, Reuss insisted, could 'justify or excuse actions by the United States or allied forces which sink to this level. Murder or torture of prisoners is horrible and un-American.' The next day, Wheeler replied to Reuss; his letter was immediately leaked to *The New York Times*, by Reuss, an outspoken opponent of the war. Wheeler agreed that Loan's act was dreadful, but that it had occurred 'in a flash of outrage rather than 'in cold blood.'' It would be inaccurate to insist that every senior White House official was shaken by violent television images. For example, National Security Advisor Walt Rostow was proud of ignoring television news, which he considered a waste of time. Rostow told me that Lyndon Johnson had installed three television monitors in his White House office so Rostow could watch the three evening news broadcasts simultaneously, but that he had made a point of not watching. He claimed to have an alleged Chinese Emperor's maxim under the glass on the top of his desk: 'There are some orders of the Emperor which *must* be disobeyed.' Rostow, to be sure, was an avowed hawk, and had access to important battlefield information from the White House Situation Room which was unavailable to members of the media, and which in fact did indicate that television images of destruction hardly served as representative of the entire Tet military situation. But surviving 16mm color film shot of Rostow in the Situation Room during the first days of the Tet Offensive, hardly suggests a figure of Olympian calm either.

Debate About Images

Clearly, historians and journalists are of two minds as to what to do with including visual images, still or moving, as part of the decision-making process, and not just for Vietnam. Nobody who sees the Adams photograph or the NBC newsfilm forgets it. But one might argue that this is not the same as making the case for its connection to historical causation. Unfortunately, for the demands of visual history, many American scholars have simply deleted the Loan footage and photograph from accounts of the Vietnam War. These days, the Vietnam War may not quite be free of its emotional resonance in the minds of many Americans of a certain age, but by now a greater concern is whether or not alleged battle heroes have manufactured their battlefield heroism. 'On a Mission to Sniff Out the Fakers With Medals,' is the continuation headline for a front-page story in *The New York Times*, August 10, 2001. The reporter notes that fraud hunters have increased in number thanks to a 'surge of wartime fabrication.' The article reminds readers of Pulitzer Prize-winning historian Joseph Ellis, who regaled his students with stories of Vietnam battlefield heroism, when in actual fact he taught history at West Point and got no closer to Saigon than the Hudson River in New York.

And Vietnam remains, as Robert McMahon indicates in his 2001 presidential address to the Society of Historians of American Foreign Relations, fertile ground for 'contested memory.' McMahon, speaking to those who teach American diplomatic history at the college level, points out our society's inability to reach a consensus as to what is or is not the 'lesson' of the Vietnam War. His thoughtful comments about memory are well-taken, both by those inside America, and scholars abroad who hope to place the Vietnam War within an appropriate historical context. Unfortunately, for those interested in media images, McMahon is more willing to speak of blockbuster Hollywood films than of television. Indeed, it seems that McMahon is only prepared to mention the continued relevance of a thirteen-part Public Broadcasting System series, *Vietnam: A Television History*, produced many years ago, in conjunction with a companion book by Stanley Karnow. McMahon slips past the shortcomings of the PBS series by relegating criticism to two slight articles which suggest that the critics of the series are simply crackpots—the proof being a connection with Accuracy in Media, a conservative media organization [which lot is purpose] with the collapse of communism.

Contested Historical Memory

The question of media impact has great significance for students of policy-making, for whom the presumed 'lessons' of the Vietnam War have considerable attraction. It is not true, for example, that in general television news reports were unfavourable to an Administration point of view. Most television coverage of the war was visually uninteresting; television's impact was overrated; the 'living-room war' is a remembered fiction. Television followed elite opinion; it did not lead.

But there is an exception to the rule, and that is the Loan execution photograph and newsfilm. It is impossible to separate the one from the other, particularly since television in America and Britain ran the still photograph and on NBC the still photograph appeared one evening; the color newsfilm of the same incident the next night. The Loan execution is the most visually significant footage to come out of the war; it merits careful attention precisely because it defines the potential of the medium for influencing elite and mass opinion. Its meaning is not simply found in, as it were, the aesthetic qualities of violence. Its impact is found by placing these images of violence within a particular context in which these images first appeared.

In early 1968 American citizens, Administration leaders, and elite opinion had become uneasy about Johnson's ill-conceived public relations campaign. Johnson needed progress; he has fighting an undeclared war, and public opposition was growing, as suggested by the March on the Pentagon in October 1967. There had to be 'light at the end of the tunnel' or the 'credibility gap' would turn into a chasm. The disbelief was already there. Into this critical situation came the dramatic North Vietnamese military action we remember as the Tet Offensive. It seemed that rosy prognostications were totally incorrect. It seemed that all South Vietnam was about to fall to the North Vietnamese. And the military action was particularly obvious in down Saigon, the largest city in all of Vietnam, the South Vietnamese capital city, and the place where all news organizations housed their employees. In this moment of doubt and uncertainty, a visual microcosm purporting to show the actual practice of justice by the government of South Vietnam offered persuasive-albeit misleading-evidence which gave people looking for factual reasons to justify a change in policy an opportunity to do so. The Loan footage and photograph legitimized the moral arguments of the anti-war movement. In this moment of crisis, a television news story and a still photograph became part of the foreign policy-making process for the average person, for the politician looking for dramatic images with which to clothe his election-year promises, and for policy-makers, both military and civilian. There is a visual component to the Vietnam War in early 1968. American policy became clear with Johnson's 31 March 1968 speech. The unique confluence of extraordinary visual imagery and extraordinary policy uncertainty makes the Loan photograph and newsfilm a significant part of America's move from hawk to dove in early 1968. It is a part of contested historical memory which historians simply must confront.

Lessons Learned from Media Violence

Robert M. Liebert, Emily S. Davidson, and John M. Neale

This article by psychologists Robert Liebert, Emily Davidson, and John Neale summarizes the research as of the mid-1970s on children and the effects of media violence. They observe that opinions as well as research with varying degrees of sophistication have tackled the question and there is a wide range of answers about how media violence affects children.

Liebert and colleagues highlight the studies revealing the extent to which children learn by observation and then poses questions about the relevance of this research to the media violence issue. They also discuss research that shows a yearly increase in violence on television and research that assesses the frequency with which children view media violence. Lastly, the authors analyze the lessons about norms and behavior that television violence teaches.

Liebert, professor of psychology at SUNY Stony Brook until his passing in 2002, was the author of fourteen books. Davidson is Associate Professor of Psychology at Texas A & M University; her research and publications focus on the development of self-esteem in children. Neale is Adjunct Professor of Psychiatry at the Mount Sinai School of Medicine in New York. He is the author of numerous publications on abnormal psychology in children.

How does watching violent television programs affect children? This question has been posed continually since the advent of television sets as a common fixture in American and European homes almost two decades ago. Answers to it, based

Robert M. Liebert, Emily S. Davidson, and John M. Neale, "Aggression in Childhood: The Impact of Television," *Where Do You Draw the Line?: An Exploration into Media Violence, Pornography, and Censorship*. Provo, UT: Brigham Young University Press, 1974, pp. 113–118. Reproduced by permission.

both on simple opinion and on research which reflects varying degrees of sophistication, have ranged from confident statements that television's influence is uniformly pernicious to equally glib assertions that merely watching entertainment fare can do little to shape children's social behavior.

Summary of Psychology Research

Although literally hundreds of studies have been focused directly or indirectly on television and its effects upon youngsters, the series of investigations commissioned by the Television and Social Behavior Program of the United States National Institute of Mental Health constituted one of the first systematic and purposefully coordinated attempts to employ the efforts of a large group of researchers with relevant expertise and diverse viewpoints. As psychologists specializing in children's development—both normal and abnormal—each of us contributed to the Television and Social Behavior inquiry. This involvement gave us an opportunity, over the past few years, to read and study all of the technical documents, research reports, and summaries as they were prepared and to evaluate them in the light of past and other recent research.

For concerned citizens the task of keeping informed of this work has been unfortunately complicated by the fact that the Television and Social Behavior Program generated almost 5,000 pages of technical material; the official summary (J.H. Cisin), while considerably shorter, is clouded by the participation of five network representatives who persistently minimized the effects of television and confused the significant issues (P.M. Boffey & J. Walsh; J. Morgenstern; M.B. Paisley). A full account of the Program's work and related evidence has been presented elsewhere (R.M. Liebert, J.M. Neale, & E.S. Davidson). The purpose of this paper is to summarize briefly the state of our present knowledge as it has grown out of these and later investigations and to reflect on some possibilities for the future.

Learning by Observation

The scientific issue most fundamentally related to the particular question of the effects of television revolves around the nature of *observational learning*, the way in which the behavior of children and adults changes as a function of exposure to the behavior of others. Regardless of their other theoretical views, social scientists have virtually all acknowledged that a child's values and behavior are shaped, at least in part, by observational learning. Research has shown that the simple observation of others can be very potent in changing such widely varied aspects of social behavior as a child's willingness to aid others, his ability to display self-control, and his learning of language. Young children's observation of others on film has been shown to increase sharing and to markedly reduce fear reactions—if, of course, the content is designed to teach these lessons.

This list represents only a few examples from the impressive body of evidence which suggests that learning by observation is a critical aspect of the social learning processes through which the child is informed about the world around him and molded into an adult member of his society. It is in this context that social scientists asked whether viewing violent television entertainment has a significant impact on the young. In answering, they had to consider four points: How much violence is shown on television? How much violent entertainment is actually seen by children? What do they learn from this exposure? And, finally: Does such learning lead to changes in real-life behavior?

Increasing Violence

Although violence has always been part of American entertainment in television, its frequency has increased steadily over the past twenty years. In 1954, for example, violence-saturated action and adventure programming accounted for only 17% of prime time network offerings; by 1961 the figure was 60%. Translating such figures into concrete terms, during one week of television in 1960 there were 144 murders, 13 kidnappings, 7 torture scenes, 4 lynchings, and a few more miscellaneous acts of violence, all occurring before 9:00 p.m. By 1968 the National Association for Better Broadcasting estimated that the average child would watch the violent destruction of more than 13,400 persons on television between the ages of five and fifteen.

The most accurate estimate of current [1972] levels of violence on television during prime time and Saturday morning has Been provided by Gerbner et al. [Communications professor] who define violence as:

> *The overt expression of physical force against others or self, or the compelling of action against one's will on pain of being hurt or killed (1972a:34).*

In Gerbner's work, carefully trained observers watched a full week of network entertainment programs on all of the major networks, with striking results. In 1969 about eight in ten shows contained violence, and the frequency of violent episodes, as defined above, was almost eight per hour. Further, the most violent programs of all were those designed exclusively for children—cartoons.

> *The average cartoon hour in 1967 contained more than three times as many violent episodes as the average dramatic hour. The trend toward shorter plays sandwiched between frequent commercials on fast moving cartoon programs further increased the saturation. In 1969, with a violent episode at least every two minutes on all Saturday morning cartoon programming (including the least violent and including commercial time), ... the average cartoon hour had nearly six times the violence rate of the average adult television drama hour, and nearly twelve times the rate of the average movie hour.*

Gerbner has continued his analysis of network television dramas, and the data for 1970 and 1971 have recently been made available. He summarizes the new findings: "... New programs in 1971 spearheaded the trend toward more lethal killers by depicting record high proportions of screen killers" (1972b:3)....

... Clearly, violence on television is not decreasing at any appreciable rate. Prime time drama was still, in the 1971–72 season, overwhelmingly violent. The new figures are of special interest since they reflect a long history of unfulfilled network promises. In the mid 1960s network officials had promised a sharp decrease in TV violence and then claimed that the promise had been met. Gerbner's 1967 and 1968 data showed that it had not. The promise was reissued, but, again, the appearance of Gerbner's 1969 data ... showed little change. It was then claimed that substantial changes had certainly occurred during the 1970 to 1971 seasons. Now, again, the facts have answered with unfortunate monotony: little change.

Frequency of Viewing Violence

Portrayals of violence on television cannot produce an effect unless they are seen. Therefore, we must ask about the frequency with which children actually view such shows. An extensive survey of media uses among more than one thousand children from widely varied backgrounds. The [study] concluded that "television saturation was almost total; only 2% of the students stated that there was not a working TV set in their home." The data also showed that more than one-third of the first-graders are still watching television at 8:30 p.m. on weeknights, and more than one-half of the sixthgraders are doing so. Likewise, psychologists A.H. Stein & L.K. Friedrich (1972) reported that in a sample of about 100 preschool children, television viewing was among the most frequently reported waking activities. Indeed, exposure to television is, for children, so pervasive that psychologist G.S. Lesser (1970) contends that a child born today will, by the age of 18, have spent more of his life watching television than in any other single activity but sleep.

The impact of television can be seen even more clearly by moving from percentage figures to absolute numbers. Psychologists J.J. McIntyre & J.J. Teevan (1972), citing the Violence Commission staff reports of 1969, remind us that "on one Monday during the period covered, over five million children under the age of 12 . . . were still watching between 10:30 and 11:00 p.m. . . ." They also point to the Commission's observations that "there is a great deal of violent content available, at all times of the day, for all manner of intended audience."

Moreover, cartoons, the most violent of all types of TV entertainment, are among those most often watched by young children. In the Lyle and Hoffman reports, for example, 24% of the first grade children said that cartoons were their favorite type of program. A similar pattern was found in Stein and Friedrich's study of preschoolers, whose parents reported that they watched cartoons an average of more than seven hours per week; even adult violent programs were watched more than a full hour per week by these three-to-five-year-old children.

It is important to note, though, that high exposure to violence is more a result of saturation by broadcasters than a strong preference for this type of programming by youngsters. Among first graders, for example, the two most popular programs are situation comedies ("My Favorite Martian" and "I Love Lucy"); preschoolers prefer "Sesame Street" to violent cartoons.

TV Violence - Lessons Learned

There is little doubt that children can learn novel forms of behavior—both words and actions—from simply watching others. It is, however, only through systematic research that we are able to see the degree to which this form of learning is effectively mediated by television and televisionlike formats.

Studies by A. Bandura, designed to show that brief exposure to novel *aggressive* behaviors can lead to their acquisition by quite young children, have uniformly shown that this influence is potent indeed. In one study, for example, 88% of the children (three-to-five-year-old boys and girls) who saw an aggressive television program displayed imitative aggression in a play situation even though they had not been asked to do so and were free to play with attractive, nonaggressive toys such as a tea set, crayons, cars and trucks, plastic farm animals, and the like.

Further, there is evidence that behavior acquired in this way may be recalled for long periods of time. Psychologist D.J. Hicks found that children shown a simulated television program similar to those used by Bandura and his associates learned many new aggressive behaviors after a single viewing and could still produce them when tested again, without further exposure, six months later. So there is no doubt that children learn, with the level of repeated exposure which takes place, a good deal of the aggressive repertoire that they see in televised violence.

Beyond teaching specific ways of perpetrating aggression and mayhem, contemporary TV entertainment conveys a more general lesson: violence succeeds. In an early investigation O.N. Larsen, L.N. Gray, & J.G. Fortis, for example, eighteen programs were studied, six in each of three categories: adult programs, "kidult" programs (programs where the child or teenage audience comprises at least 30% of the total audience), and children's programs—usually cartoons. In all three program types, violent methods were the ones most frequently used in goal attainment. And, when goal achievement methods were further analyzed for degree of success, it became clear that the most successful methods were *not* those in the socially approved category. Simply, then, television programming—aimed both at children and at adults—is presenting an antisocial system of values.

Network officials, though, have sometimes justified television violence because the "bad guy" is usually punished for his misdeeds. The argument deserves a closer look. The usual sequence involves aggression or other anti-social behavior by the villain, through which he achieves his immediate objectives (the plans for the latest missile or the crown jewels of England). Next, the hero catches up with and vanquishes the villain—by virtue of exemplary performance in the final brawl or shoot-out. The hero's reward is a raise, a blonde, or a bottle of champagne; if he is lucky, he may get all three plus a vacation in the sun. The lesson is thus that aggression, while reprehensible in criminals, is acceptable for those who have right on their side. But all of us, children and adults, rich and poor, on any side of any legal statute, feel we have right on *our* side. "Every man," William Saroyan wrote many years ago, "is a good man in a bad world—as he himself knows."

A Lack of Consensus on the Effects of Media Violence

Media Awareness Network

The following article published by the Media Awareness Network summarizes research from the 1950s through the early 1990s on media violence and its effects.

The article notes that a variety of conclusions have been drawn from the many studies conducted; as a result, there is a lack of consensus on the issue. Nevertheless, several research strands have been derived, such as the link between media violence consumption and aggression in children, the notion of increased risks for violence-viewing children to manifest aggressive behavior as adults, and the idea that the introduction of television into a community contributes to violent behavior. By reporting the many findings on media violence effects, the report underscores the multidimensional complexity of the issue.

Incorporated in 1996, the Media Awareness Network is a non-profit organization that helps develop media literacy programs as a means of educating people in the use of critical thinking skills.

Whether or not exposure to media violence causes increased levels of aggression and violence in young people is the perennial question of media effects research. Some experts, like University of Michigan professor L. Rowell Huesmann, argue that fifty years of evidence show "that exposure to media violence causes children to behave more aggressively and affects them as adults years later." Others, like Jonathan Freedman of the University of Toronto, maintain that "the scientific evidence simply does not show that watching violence either produces violence in people, or desensitizes them to it."

Media Awareness Network, "Research on the Effects of Media Violence," *www.media-awareness.ca*. Copyright © 2007 Media Awareness Network. Reproduced with permission.

Lack of Consensus

Andrea Martinez at the University of Ottawa conducted a comprehensive review of the scientific literature for the Canadian Radio-television and Telecommunications Commission (CRTC) in 1994. She concluded that the lack of consensus about media effects reflects three "grey areas" or constraints contained in the research itself.

First, media violence is notoriously hard to define and measure. Some experts who track violence in television programming, such as George Gerbner of Temple University, define violence as the act (or threat) of injuring or killing someone, independent of the method used or the surrounding context. Accordingly, Gerbner includes cartoon violence in his data-set. But others, such as University of Laval professors Guy Paquette and Jacques de Guise, specifically exclude cartoon violence from their research because of its comical and unrealistic presentation.

Second, researchers disagree over the type of relationship the data supports. Some argue that exposure to media violence causes aggression. Others say that the two are associated, but that there is no causal connection. (That both, for instance, may be caused by some third factor.) And others say the data supports the conclusion that there is no relationship between the two at all.

Third, even those who agree that there is a connection between media violence and aggression disagree about how the one effects the other. Some say that the mechanism is a psychological one, rooted in the ways we learn. For example, Huesmann argues that children develop "cognitive scripts" that guide their own behaviour by imitating the actions of media heroes. As they watch violent shows, children learn to internalize scripts that use violence as an appropriate method of problem-solving.

Other researchers argue that it is the physiological effects of media violence that cause aggressive behaviour. Exposure to violent imagery is linked to increased heart rate, faster respiration and higher blood pressure. Some think that this simulated "fight-or-flight" response predisposes people to act aggressively in the real world.

Still others focus on the ways in which media violence primes or cues pre-existing aggressive thoughts and feelings. They argue that an individual's desire to strike out is justified by media images in which both the hero and the villain use violence to seek revenge, often without consequences.

In her final report to the CRTC, Martinez concluded that most studies support "a positive, though weak, relation between exposure to television violence and aggressive behaviour." Although that relationship cannot be "confirmed systematically," she agrees with Dutch researcher Tom Van der Voot who argues that it would be illogical to conclude that "a phenomenon does not exist simply because it is found at times not to occur, or only to occur under certain circumstances."

Violence-Viewing and Aggression

The lack of consensus about the relationship between media violence and real-world aggression has not impeded ongoing research. Here's a sampling of conclusions drawn to date, from the various research strands:

Research strand: Children who consume high levels of media violence are more likely to be aggressive in the real world

In 1956, researchers took to the laboratory to compare the behaviour of 24 children watching TV. Half watched a violent episode of the cartoon *Woody Woodpecker*, and the other 12 watched the non-violent cartoon *The Little Red Hen*. During play afterwards, the researchers observed that the children who watched the violent cartoon were much more likely to hit other children and break toys.

Six years later, in 1963, professors A. Badura, D. Ross and S.A. Ross studied the effect of exposure to real-world violence, television violence, and cartoon violence. They divided 100 preschool children into four groups. The first group watched a real person shout insults at an inflatable doll while hitting it with a mallet. The second group watched the incident on television. The third watched a cartoon version of the same scene, and the fourth watched nothing.

When all the children were later exposed to a frustrating situation, the first three groups responded with more aggression than the control group. The children who watched the incident on television were just as aggressive as those who had watched the real person use the mallet; and both were more aggressive than those who had only watched the cartoon.

Over the years, laboratory experiments such as these have consistently shown that exposure to violence is associated with increased heartbeat, blood pressure and respiration rate, and a greater willingness to administer electric shocks to inflict pain or punishment on others. However, this line of enquiry has been criticized because of its focus on short term results and the artificial nature of the viewing environment.

Other scientists have sought to establish a connection between media violence and aggression outside the laboratory. For example, a number of surveys indicate that children and young people who report a preference for violent entertainment also score higher on aggression indexes than those who watch less violent shows. L. Rowell Huesmann reviewed studies conducted in Australia, Finland, Poland, Israel, Netherlands and the United States. He reports, "the child most likely to be aggressive would be the one who (a) watches violent television programs most of the time, (b) believes that these shows portray life just as it is, [and] (c) identifies strongly with the aggressive characters in the shows. . . ."

Effects into Adulthood

Research Strand: Children who watch high levels of media violence are at increased risk of aggressive behaviour as adults

In 1960, University of Michigan Professor Leonard Eron studied 856 grade three students living in a semi-rural community in Columbia County, New York, and found that the children who watched violent television at home behaved more aggressively in school. Eron wanted to track the effect of this exposure over the years, so he revisited Columbia County in 1971, when the children who participated in the 1960 study were 19 years of age. He found that boys who watched violent TV when they were eight were more likely to get in trouble with the law as teenagers.

When Eron and Huesmann returned to Columbia County in 1982, the subjects were 30 years old. They reported that those participants who had watched more violent TV as eight-year-olds were more likely, as adults, to be convicted of serious crimes, to use violence to discipline their children, and to treat their spouses aggressively.

Professor Monroe Lefkowitz published similar findings in 1971. Lefkowitz interviewed a group of eight-year-olds and found that the boys who watched more violent TV were more likely to act aggressively in the real world. When he interviewed the same boys ten years later, he found that the more violence a boy watched at eight, the more aggressively he would act at age eighteen.

Columbia University professor Jeffrey Johnson has found that the effect is not limited to violent shows. Johnson tracked 707 families in upstate New York for 17 years, starting in 1975. In 2002, Johnson reported that children who watched one to three hours of television each day when they were 14 to 16 years old were 60 per cent more likely to be involved in assaults and fights as adults than those who watched less TV.

Kansas State University professor John Murray concludes, "The most plausible interpretation of this pattern of correlations is that early preference for violent television programming and other media is one factor in the production of aggressive and antisocial behavior when the young boy becomes a young man."

However, this line of research has attracted a great deal of controversy. Pullitzer Prize-winning author Richard Rhodes has attacked Eron's work, arguing that his conclusions are based on an insignificant amount of data. Rhodes claims that Eron had information about the amount of TV viewed in 1960 for only 3 of the 24 men who committed violent crimes as adults years later. Rhodes concludes that Eron's work is "poorly conceived, scientifically inadequate, biased and sloppy if not actually fraudulent research."

Guy Cumberbatch, head of the Communications Research Group, a U.K. social policy think tank, has equally harsh words for Johnson's study. Cumberbatch claims Johnson's group of 88 under-one-hour TV watchers is "so small, it's aberrant." And, as journalist Ben Shouse points out, other critics say that Johnson's study "can't rule out the possibility that television is just a marker for some unmeasured environmental or psychological influence on both aggression and TV habits."

Behavioral Changes

Research Strand: The introduction of television into a community leads to an increase in violent behaviour

Researchers have also pursued the link between media violence and real life aggression by examining communities before and after the introduction of television. In the mid 1970s, University of British Columbia professor Tannis McBeth Williams studied a remote village in British Columbia both before and after television was introduced. She found that two years after TV arrived, violent incidents had increased by 160 per cent.

Researchers Gary Granzberg and Jack Steinbring studied three Cree communities in northern Manitoba during the

1970s and early 1980s. They found that four years after television was introduced into one of the communities, the incidence of fist fights and black eyes among the children had increased significantly. Interestingly, several days after an episode of *Happy Days* aired, in which one character joined a gang called the Red Demons, children in the community created rival gangs, called the Red Demons and the Green Demons, and the conflict between the two seriously disrupted the local school.

University of Washington Professor Brandon Centerwall noted that the sharp increase in the murder rate in North America in 1955 occurred eight years after television sets began to enter North American homes. To test his hypothesis that the two were related, he examined the murder rate in South Africa where, prior to 1975, television was banned by the government. He found that twelve years after the ban was lifted, murder rates skyrocketed.

University of Toronto Professor Jonathan Freedman has criticized this line of research. He points out that Japanese television has some of the most violent imagery in the world, and yet Japan has a much lower murder rate than other countries, including Canada and the United States, which have comparatively less violence on TV....

Desensitization and Reality

Research Strand: Media violence desensitizes people to real violence

A number of studies in the 1970's showed that people who are repeatedly exposed to media violence tend to be less disturbed when they witness real world violence, and have less sympathy for its victims. For example, Professors V.B. Cline, R.G. Croft, and S. Courrier studied young boys over a two-year period. In 1973, they reported that boys who watch more than 25 hours of television per week are significantly less likely to be aroused by real world violence than those boys who watch 4 hours or less per week. . . .

. . . Research Strand: People who watch a lot of media violence tend to believe that the world is more dangerous than it is in reality

George Gerbner has conducted the longest running study of television violence. His seminal research suggests that heavy TV viewers tend to perceive the world in ways that are consistent with the images on TV. As viewers' perceptions of the world come to conform with the depictions they see on TV, they become more passive, more anxious, and more fearful. Gerbner calls this the "Mean World Syndrome."

Gerbner's research found that those who watch greater amounts of television are more likely to:

- overestimate their risk of being victimized by crime

- believe their neighbourhoods are unsafe

- believe "fear of crime is a very serious personal problem"

- assume the crime rate is increasing, even when it is not

CHAPTER 3

Media Violence in the 1990s and Beyond

Chapter Preface

The issue of violence in the media was renewed with fervor in the 1990s as videogames, music lyrics, and the Internet came under scrutiny. This, combined with envelope-pushing in the film and television industry, also led to the creation of several advocacy groups in the mid-1990s.

Real-life events in the 1990s amplified the debate above all else. Tragedies such as the Columbine shooting in 1999 factored significantly into the debate. On April 20, 1999, two students at Columbine High School in Littleton, Colorado shot and killed twelve students and one teacher. Twenty-four others were wounded in the massacre, in which the perpetrators also killed themselves. At the time, it was the second-deadliest school shooting in U.S. history.

A Gallup poll taken approximately one month after the Columbine tragedy found that 32 percent of Americans believe that parental responsibility could have prevented the events. Violence in the media, however, was not deemed an "important cause" by respondents. Other cultural observers disagreed.

Questions about influences quickly arose in the aftermath of the tragedy. The issue of violence in the media—television, films, video games, the growing Internet—slid under the microscope. The roles of parents and school administrators also became fodder for public debate, and investigations into "bullying" and "outsider status" added complexity to the underlying problem: What manifested this school violence and who was responsible for it?

Efforts to determine causes both cultural and immediate resulted in a widely cast net of blame that continues to the present day, with events such as the Virginia Tech shooting in April 2007—eight years later—still leaving behind more questions than answers.

Media violence remains a subject of analysis and controversy. No one has been able to prove a direct link between media violence and violent acts. Perhaps more importantly, no one has been able to disprove the indirect link.

Legal and Ethical Challenges to Violence Imagery in the News

Wendy Lesser

In the following excerpt, Wendy Lesser delves into the general public's fascination with murder. She claims that the question of media violence and its effects on behavior has neither been resolved nor is likely to disappear. Thus, her concern is not to investigate the effects of media violence but rather to consider why society has an interest in watching violence. She addresses fictional murder and real-life murder as well as how (and whether) society perceives the distinctions between the two.

Lesser is a writer and the founding editor of The Threepenny Review, *a literary magazine. She is the author of six books of nonfiction.*

I am interested in our interest in murder. Specifically, I am drawn to the increasingly blurry borderline between real murder and fictional murder, between murder as news and murder as art, between event and story. I say "increasingly," but it is not clear that these categories were ever easily separable. Plato, in his complaint about the mimetic poets and tragedians, was convinced that their stories had a practical, often negative effect on the behavior of their audiences. His rationale for banning poets from the ideal republic—"the imitative poet produces a bad regime in the soul of each private man by making phantoms that are very far removed from the truth and by gratifying the soul's foolish part . . . . it succeeds in maiming even the decent men"—has been used ever since to object to violent or otherwise offensive art. One hears ech-

Wendy Lesser, "What Draws Us," *Pictures at an Execution*. Cambridge, MA: Harvard University Press, 1993, pp. 1–5, 7–8. Copyright © 1993 by Wendy Lesser. All rights reserved. Reprinted by permission of the publisher.

oes of it in the anxieties that gave rise to the 1986 Meese Commission on Pornography or in the even more recent feminist denunciations of violently pornographic art. None of the high-minded commissions assigned to investigate the connection between spectatorship and violent behavior has been able to come up with a causal link, despite the fact that this was the one thing they all desperately wanted to demonstrate, but the question is constantly raised anew. It is not a question that seems likely either to be resolved or to disappear; we have always been worried that made-up stories might give rise to undesirable activities.

Our Interest in Murder

But there is something new, I think, in our increasing tendency to move in the opposite direction: to convert real-world murder into made-up stories, or into artworks that offer the same satisfactions as made-up stories. Works like Truman Capote's *In Cold Blood*, Norman Mailer's *The Executioner's Song*, Errol Morris's *The Thin Blue Line*, and Janet Malcolm's *The Journalist and the Murderer* characterize our era. In the course of drawing on real murders to feed our wish for narrative, they also comment on our preoccupation with murder stories. Even the movie *The Silence of the Lambs*, garishly and self-proclaimedly theatrical as it was, seemed eerily connected to reality, referring backward to the 1950s crimes of Ed Gein—a killer who skinned and stuffed his female victims—and, more surprisingly, forward to Jeffrey Dahmer, whose cannibalistic antics hit the little screens only a few months after Hannibal Lecter's reached the big ones.

My delight in Hannibal Lecter, or in Anthony Hopkins's portrayal of Hannibal Lecter, and my more guarded, more disgusted and perhaps self-disgusted, but still admissible curiosity about Jeffrey Dahmer, do not set me apart as an eccentric in late-twentieth-century America. On the contrary. We all seem to be interested in murderers these days. They are our truth and our fiction; they are our truth as fiction, and vice versa. I want to ask ... why that should be so.

I don't intend to ask the question about what effect the witnessing of murder—in books, in movies, on television, in the newspapers, whether real or fictional or somewhere in between—has on our collective or individual behavior. I doubt that it can be answered, and in any case the tools for even attempting to answer it lie far beyond my reach, in realms where sociologists rush in. It seems to me that the kind of experiment needed to demonstrate a causal connection between spectatorship and violent behavior would, if accurately conducted, be so morally reprehensible as to invalidate the results.

Asking Other Questions

But that particular question is not the only one worth asking about the connection between art and murder. There are questions about murder that can be asked and answered by a person sitting alone at a desk. This book is not a work of philosophy, nor is it a work of literary criticism; but it will be asking the kinds of questions that are asked, or used to be asked, by philosophers, and it will be using the techniques and materials of literary criticism in an attempt to answer them. Why are we drawn to murder, as an act and as a spectacle? Who in the murder story are we drawn to—the victim, the murderer, the detective? Why, in particular, are we so interested in *seeing* murder, either enacted or caught in the act? What are the sources of pleasure in a murder story, and how do those kinds of pleasure connect with any sense of the morally suspect or reprehensible? *Is* it morally reprehensible to take an interest in murder, and is it possible to talk about such things without sounding either self-righteous or sleazy?

I take the word "interest" to be the appropriate one here, signaling, in its opposition to "disinterest," our involvement in the subject, our complicity in its ethical implications. (This is not to disparage disinterestedness; we may need to bring to bear our best efforts at disinterested analysis if we are to uncover the nature of our interest.) I also view "interest" as appropriately understated: "fascination" or "obsession," while accurate for some, overstates the general case, while modifiers like "ghoulish" and "depraved" tilt the argument unfairly from the beginning. The question of whether there is indeed anything wrong with such an interest is part of what I hope to explore.

The answer to this question seems simple if we apply it to, say, mystery novels. Very few people would condemn the readers of murder mysteries as depraved or ghoulish or otherwise morally inadequate. But the question gains more pressure, more immediacy, the further we move away from the neatly contrived and the artificially resolvable. In particular, the question seems to alter as we move from the realm of fiction to the realm of the explicitly real. If it is acceptable to be interested in fictional murders, is it equally or similarly acceptable to be interested in real ones? Why does it matter that we be able to tell the difference between real and fictional murders? Ought our interest in seeing a murder enacted be allowed to extend to watching someone killed before our very eyes?

Broadcasting an Execution

This is not a merely hypothetical question. In 1991, a trial held in San Francisco asked, and temporarily answered, the question of whether a television station should be allowed to record and broadcast the execution of a condemned man in the California gas chamber. That legal case, *KQED v. Daniel B. Vasquez*, will provide the central framework of my discussion in this book, for in the course of the trial there emerged all sorts of information and ideas about how we respond to murder as spectacle. At present, in America, any state-run execution will be that of a murderer, since murder, for at least the last two decades, has been the only crime for which civilians are put to death. An execution is itself the only kind of murder that is planned and publicly announced in advance, so that we know exactly who the victim will be and when he will die. It is thus the only form of murder that anyone but the murderer and the victim could count on attending. (Come to think of it, anyone but the murderer; the victim always has to be there too, but, except in the case of executions, he won't *count* on it in advance.) As a killing carried out in all our names, an act of the state in which we by proxy participate, it is also the only form of murder that directly implicates even the witnesses, the bystanders.

Supporters of capital punishment, and even some of its opponents, will want to argue at this point that execution is not equivalent to murder. I agree that they are not identical categories. Some kinds of murder, particularly those enacted in the heat of passion, bear no external resemblance to executions, which are by definition planned and coldblooded. Some executions—of Nazi concentration-camp directors, for instance, or professional torturers—might be viewed by most people as "justified"; but then, some private murders—those committed in self-defense, or in response to extreme abuse—are also described that way. We tend to say that if a killing is justified, it is not murder. But the definition of what is justifiable alters over time. The fact that the majority supports something, as eighty percent of Californians and more than half of all Americans are presently said to support capital punishment, does not mean that it can be justified in moral terms; the majority used to support slave-owning, vigilante lynching, hand-removal for stealing, and other forms of torture that we now consider barbaric. For my purposes, execution shares enough of the characteristics of murder to be counted as part of the general category: it includes a victim who does not want to die, and an agent that nonetheless kills him. And execution has special characteristics—in particular, that it can be watched, and *is* watched—which make it more accessible than most other kinds of murder. . . .

Death as Theater

. . . As you may have gathered, I do not approve of the death penalty, and that attitude will naturally color my coverage of *KQED v. Vasquez*. It will not, however, determine my response to the central question in the case—whether executions should be televised or not—for there were critics of capital punishment on both sides. Some death-penalty opponents insisted that televising executions would cause people to vote against capital punishment, others that these broadcasts would only arouse the population's bloodlust. I don't know which, if either, of these predictions is the correct one; as I said, the effects of art and media on behavior are not my concern here. What I find useful in the legal case is the way it opens up and clarifies some of the other questions that concern me about our interest in murder.

Specifically, the case of *KQED v. Vasquez* points up the crucial connection between murder and theater—between death imposed on a human being by another human being, and dramatic spectacle. This connection is not limited to murder's inclusion as a plot device in theater, though that is importantly there, from Agamemnon's, Clytemnestra's, and Orestes' murders of their various family members, through Shakespeare's tragedies and the bloody Jacobean dramas, to that debased modern version, the murder-mystery play that runs for years if not decades on Broadway or in the West End. Nor am I referring only to the theoretical overlap between theater's way of working on its audience and the fascinations of violent spectacle, though that too is there, in Artaud's elaborations of his Theater of Cruelty, in Brecht's discussions of his "alienation effect," and in other analyses of drama's assaultive function. All these connections remind us that there is a profound and historical link between murder and theater. But what has especially struck me, in thinking about *KQED v. Vasquez*, is the way the murderer takes on the role of the central performer in his plot, converting us by default into audience members. While this figure of speech can be applied to all chronicled or broadcast murders, it is actually true in the case of an execution, where the murderer himself is murdered before the eyes of assembled spectators—where the murderer, for once, becomes a victim as well as a killer. Thinking about execution and its real or potential witnesses can help us to understand why and how we identify with the various participants in a murder story. It instructs us about the ways in which murder plays on our desire for a story that will take us out of ourselves. It allows us to focus on our suspicions about the reliability of sense data and visual evidence. It also offers us new realizations about the link between pleasure and horror.

More Ethical Questions

My questions and concerns about murder don't fit neatly into the subdisciplines—ethics, aesthetics, epistemology—that philosophers have devised for us. Rather, my investigations suggest that these areas overlap in important ways, so that some of our pressing ethical questions (for instance: How much should we be allowed to indulge our interest in and curiosity about murder in the face of another person's death? What harm, to the murdered person or to ourselves, do we do by using someone's murder as the occasion for our entertainment or instruction?) can be answered in part by exploring aesthetic questions (How does art work on us, and in what ways does fictional art differ from "true-life" art or unshaped life?) and epistemological questions (How do we take in and interpret information if we are present at an event, as opposed to seeing it on television or in a movie or reading about it in a novel or a newspaper? How is experience mediated, and how do different kinds of mediation make themselves felt to us?). Murder, as a subject, makes us especially aware that such questions, like their answers, do not fit into one philosophical division or another, but cut across divisions.

Videogames Teach Children How to Shoot Guns

Clive Thompson

The following article by Clive Thompson documents his personal experience testing a theory about the effects of media violence. The author talks with Dave Grossman, a military man with a psychology degree who has publicly asserted that videogames and the ability to shoot a gun are closely connected. Grossman insists that children who have never used a gun before can do so with unusual accuracy if they have simulated similar experiences through videogames. The author, who has played videogames most of his life but who has never held a gun, conducts the interview at a shooting range where he is about to test Grossman's theory.

Thompson discovers that he was able to hit his range target with surprising accuracy. In addition to discussing youth violence, military training methods, and the videogame debate, the author offers reflections on the significance of his experience— and what it does and does not imply. He concludes that the debate about videogame violence is frustrating because it is too complex for simple answers.

Thompson has written science and technology articles for numerous magazines, including The New York Times Magazine, Wired, *and* Details.

The sun beats down like a hammer on the Mississippi firing range as Lt.-Col. Dave Grossman crouches on the ground. The heat is furious and he's beginning to sweat a bit, his army crew cut glistening as he punches in the combination to open his safety box. Inside are two guns. Grossman pulls out a .22-caliber pistol.

Clive Thompson, "Good Clean Fun," *Shift Magazine*, December, 1999. Copyright © 1999 by Clive Thompson. Reproduced by permission.

Videogames and Killing Ability

This, he tells me, is the same model that fourteen-year-old Michael Carneal stole from his neighbor's house in Paducah, Kentucky, on December 1, 1997. Carneal took the gun to a high-school prayer meeting and opened fire on the group. "He fired eight shots and got eight hits on eight different kids. He killed three and paralyzed one for life," Grossman notes grimly in his slight Arkansas accent. It was an astonishing piece of marksmanship—a hit ratio that many highly trained police officers can't achieve. Last year, for example, four experienced New York City cops shot at unarmed Amadou Diallo, firing forty-one bullets from barely fifteen feet away; fewer than half hit their mark.

But perhaps more startling about Carneal is another salient fact: He'd never shot a handgun before. "So how did he get such incredible aim?" Grossman asks. "Where did he get that killing ability?"

His answer: videogames. In a controversial book out this fall, *Stop Teaching Our Kids to Kill*, the forty-three-year-old Grossman details how Carneal had trained for hours and hours on point-and-shoot games. The teenager had practiced killing literally thousands of people virtually; he'd learned to aim for the head in order to dispatch each victim with just one shot.

Videogames have long been blamed for provoking violence, but rarely by someone of Grossman's background and expertise. A military man and Pulitzer-nominated authority on the psychology of killing, Grossman shot to prominence after the Columbine school massacre. In countless media appearances, he has argued that modern videogames are eerily similar to the training tools that military and law enforcement agencies use to teach soldiers and officers to kill. Kids learn these skills, he writes in his book, "much the same way as the astronauts on Apollo 11 learned how to fly to the moon without ever leaving the ground." The proof, he argues, is in the profusion of mass high-school shootings in recent years, where kids with limited experience in using guns have displayed excellent aim and tactical maneuvers, not to mention a view of murder as fun.

I am here to test Grossman's theory. I have never even held a gun, let alone fired one. But for two decades, I've been avidly playing videogames, including the wickedly violent arcade shooters that Grossman considers the most military-like "murder simulators." I'm particularly good at these—I can usually finish Area 51 or Time Crisis for only about three bucks in quarters. If Grossman is right, I should be as deadly as Michael Carneal.

I look down the range at my target, a human-shaped silhouette. It's twenty feet away, roughly the same distance from which Carneal shot his victims. In the blazing heat sweat drips slowly down the small of my back.

I raise the barrel of the gun.

The Videogame Debate

The videogame debate has been going on for years, but Grossman has arguably brought it to a new level. He is a peculiar combination of ultra-pundit (known for his crisp sound bites on violence) and career soldier. Unlike other critics, who typically hail from the media-literacy or family-values camps, he has direct experience in the domain of killing. During his twenty-three-year stint in the army (from which he retired in 1998), he participated in the Panama invasion. He has taught the psychology of killing ("killology") at the West Point military academy and the University of Arkansas. Today, as founder and director of the Killology Research Group in Arkansas, he works full time training police officers—and remains an enthusiastic ambassador of military culture. He says "roger" and "check" instead of "OK," and calls everyone "brother."

Grossman's epiphany about videogames came through a circuitous route. Research for his psychology PhD eventually became the source of his 1995 book On Killing, which examines a little-known aspect of war: that soldiers, even highly trained ones, are profoundly resistant to shooting people.

As Grossman points out, surveys of World War II veterans show that eighty percent of riflemen never once fired a gun during active combat, even when enemy bullets were flying around them. During the American Civil War, according to data collected after battles, many soldiers only pretended to fire their weapons, loading them again and again without actually discharging a shot. On some level, it seems, they simply couldn't bear the prospect of shooting other human beings. Had they done so, casualties would have obviously been much higher.

Faced with armies full of reluctant gunners, the U.S. military began devising new techniques to definitively train men to shoot-and shoot to kill. The answer lay in classic "operant conditioning" methods made famous by American psychologist B.F. Skinner in the fifties. In a series of experiments, Skinner trained rats to push on a bar, after which they were rewarded with food. Positive or negative reinforcement, he argued, could make any form of activity virtually automatic, overriding conscious objections.

Military Training via Simulation

For the military, this meant setting up realistic shooting simulations. Soldiers were put into mock combat situations, filled with noise and riot; they were taught to fire at pop-up silhouettes until it became a twitch instinct. The conditioning worked well. By the Korean War, Grossman found, such training brought the firing ratio up to fifty-five percent. In Vietnam, the number skyrocketed to ninety-five percent.

In the eighties, the armed forces began using an even more powerful and cheaper training tool: video- and computer-graphics-based simulations. Many were modeled directly on videogames. One popular military sim was a barely-modified version of the early Nintendo game Duck Hunt.

Which is when Grossman began to look away from the battlefields and into the arcades. If the army was using game-like sims to train its killers, were the arcades doing the same thing, inadvertently, to youth?

An incendiary chapter in his 1995 book blames Hollywood violence and the rise of super-realistic videogames for the seismic increase of "serious assault" cases in the U.S.— which had nearly doubled between 1977 and 1993, from 240 to 440 incidents per 100,000 people. In Grossman's analysis, different forms of entertainment provide different elements of violence training. Hollywood and TV desensitize youth to the consequences of violence, a proposition generally backed by study after study. More controversial is the role he assigns to videogames as teachers of gun-handling skills. It is a theory supported by scant scientific evidence; Grossman bases his claims entirely on military research and his personal experience. In his own pistol-training classes at West Point, he says, some recruits displayed an uncanny facility with weapons. "Out of every class of about twenty kids, you'll often get one or two that are extraordinary shots but who'd never fired a gun before. And almost without fail, if you ask them, Where did you get to be such a good pistol shot?, they'll look you in the eye and say, Duck Hunt. Or Time Crisis. The skills transfer over immediately."

Real-Life Violence

Still, for all their explosiveness, Grossman's ideas would probably languish in obscurity if not for the Michael Carneals of the world.

High-school shootings in the U.S. have been going on for years. In fact, the 1992 to 1993 academic year was the worst in sheer numbers, with nearly fifty deaths. But they were almost all one-on-one incidents, either revenge- or gang-related. In 1997, however, the peculiarly large-scale shootings began, during which the killers fired indiscriminately at groups of people they barely knew. Consider a partial list: In October 1997, Luke Woodham shot up his high school in Pearl, Mississippi, killing two and injuring seven. A few months later, Carneal went on his prayer-group rampage. In March 1998, two kids opened fire on a school in Jonesboro, Arkansas, killing five and injuring ten. Not long after, a student in Springfield, Oregon, cut loose in a crowded cafeteria, murdering two and injuring eighteen. And then came the most violent one of all—the April 1999 shootings at Columbine, which left a stunning thirteen dead and twenty injured.

Grossman figured his prophecy was coming true. It had also hit home. In a brutal coincidence, he actually lives in Jonesboro, across town from where its school shootings occurred; he was even summoned to the middle school to help counsel traumatized teachers. The ensuing weeks and months saw Grossman appear regularly in the media, from *60 minutes* to *The New York Times*. An expert strategist, he decided the time was ripe to strike. This summer, he and co-author Gloria DeGaetano (a media literacy consultant) quickly completed work on *Stop Teaching Our Kids to Kill*, which slams violent games, movies and TV, and demands that they be legally restricted to adults only. Grossman has also trained lawyers nationwide in how to launch class-action suits against videogame companies on behalf of families whose children are killed in school shootings, as well as consulting on draft laws for videogames. The ripple effects are already here: This spring, the parents of three of Michael Carneal's victims sued, among others, several videogame companies that they felt had incited the rampage.

Now, as the media prepare for still more shootings, Grossman has arguably become the most prominent player in the videogame debate. "This whole industry is going down, and going down hard," he says with conviction.

But a question remains: Is he right?

Experiencing the Real Thing

I take a deep breath and start firing like mad, squeezing the trigger again and again until my finger aches, blasting round after round. Things are looking good: My aim is steady, my heart rate low. As I fire, bodies drop on impact—chunks of flesh flying off in all directions.

It's the day before my meeting with Grossman, and I've decided to go for a warm-up at a local arcade in Pearl, the Mississippi town I've come to to speak with him. I'm holding a plastic pistol in front of Midway's House of the Dead, blowing away endless platoons of zombies. A few days before, over the phone, Grossman spoke about the sheer physicality of guns like this one—arguing that they make games like House of the Dead preternaturally similar to a Fire Arms Training Simulator, which police officers use to hone their twitch-shooting instincts. Warming up on this stuff, he'd figured, would get me "really fired up" for the main event.

Indeed, from the time I first suggested this experiment, Grossman has displayed an almost perverse enthusiasm for it. He urged me to fly down from New York the following weekend to join him in Pearl, where he was due to guest-lecture at a police sharpshooter conference (taking place just a few miles from the high school that had its own shooting in 1997).

When we meet for lunch, he pulls out ads he has collected for various videogame companies, gleefully poking fun at them. One, for Quake, features a photo of a human foot with a toe tag; the caption says, HE PRACTICED ON A PC. Another, an ad for a force-feedback joystick, reads, PSYCHIATRISTS SAY IT IS IMPORTANT TO FEEL SOMETHING WHEN YOU KILL. He slaps his thigh. "These things are mass-murder simulators—and in their own ads, they're saying so!"

I'm not so sure. I've been a long-time defender of videogames, on TV panels and in radio debates. Games need defending, I've always felt, simply because they're the chief pastime of the young, unathletic geek, a cohort with whom I feel a personal sympathy. For these kids, gaming is a crucial refuge in a teenage world that glorifies physical power and beauty. Videogame critics frequently come from outside this geek demographic—as does Grossman—and thus inevitably err in their analysis of it. They ignore, for example, the social aspect of games—the robust culture of camaraderie and information-swapping that surrounds them. Or they focus on a few gory games that comprise a small portion of the market, such as Quake. During the Columbine coverage, clueless journalists cited Doom as if it were actually a current game, when nobody I know had played it for about four years.

Experiencing Videogames

Perhaps most problematically, critics assume that players are hopeless dupes of the videogame experience—that they are unable to critically assess what they play and are doomed only to be "influenced" by it. These critics rarely look at games as pieces of a living, breathing culture. In fact, you could argue that the tongue-in-cheek irony so prevalent in shooting games and their cartoonishly over-the-top gore are more of a comment on violence than a true enactment of it. Indeed, as gaming critic J.C. Herz once noted, the gun-toting protagonists of videogames are inevitably policemen, marines or soldiers—not mercenaries or lawless killers. What sort of social comment is that? As I sit here blowing away zombies in House of the Dead, my primary reaction is, as always, to giggle. Part of the fun is simply the deep surreality of the action.

To his credit, Grossman gives these arguments their due. Sure, games are useful socially, which is why he doesn't have any problem with non-violent ones. He also sees the irony of the gorier titles. But he doesn't think young children do. "They accept it on a different level," he says.

I was skeptical of Grossman's theory, but something happened at the Pearl arcade that gave me pause. I'm halfway through a round of L.A. Machinegunners when I notice a young man in fatigues watching me. I introduce myself, and discover that he's Sgt. Scott Sargent, a U.S. military reservist out recruiting. A recruiter in an arcade? I ask him if he wants to join me for a game.

Soon, Sargent and I are merrily annihilating virtual terrorists on the streets of L.A., using throbbing, simulated machine guns. Watching him, I see that Grossman's theory seems to apply in reverse. Sargent has had extensive training on real-life weaponry, but he's never played Machinegunners until now. Nonetheless, he's astonishingly good. And Machinegunners is one of the most difficult shooters to play—my wife becomes nauseated just watching the vertiginous, rapidly shifting angles. Despite my long experience playing this game, Sargent is better than I am, racking up more kills and sustaining fewer injuries.

As the round ends, I ask him how the game compares to real life. He pauses for a second, fingering the machine-gun controls that have a simulated recoil when you fire. I've always assumed the game recoil is a pale shadow of a real one. Apparently, this is not so. "It's actually very similar to the kick of an M-16," Sargent says. "I've trained with those things for years. It feels almost exactly the same."

At the Range

The next day, training is over. I'm at the range, holding one of Grossman's pistols.

Several National Rifle Association officials and five police officers, here for a sharpshooting competition, stand in a semicircle behind me, eyeing me worriedly. I can hardly blame them: The prospect of a neophyte blasting away is clearly unsettling. It's obvious that I don't even know how to correctly hold the thing; one officer has to gently suggest a two-handed approach. He stands next to me to make sure I keep the gun pointed down-range and to tell me when to fire. Grossman looks on with excitement. "Imagine It's House of the Dead," he calls out.

After everyone is safely a few paces back, the officer gives the nod. He leans over and touches a lever on my pistol. "The safety is down," he announces. "It's ready to fire."

For a second, I feel an odd sensation of danger, as If I'm only now realizing how deadly this thing really is. It's like driving along the edge of a cliff and suddenly visualizing yourself veering off into space. I have a brief, unbidden thought that at any moment I could swivel around and shoot three or four of the cops in the gut. I banish the notion immediately, then grip the gun more firmly and focus.

Guns are a peculiarly modernist combination of form and function, which is part of their allure. They have no extraneous elements: Just point and shoot. I squint down the range at the silhouette target. I squeeze the trigger.

Bang.

A hole appears in the upper left shoulder of the target. Whoa: I've hit it squarely, though I aimed too high. I fire again, and again. I'm nervous, far more than I expected, and trembling like a leaf. Perhaps it's because five cops are staring at me. Perhaps it's because I'm trying to fire as quickly as possible, to emulate the speed of Carneal and the other teen killers, who had little time to line up their shots.

Yet for all my panic, it's quickly become apparent that I'm actually doing quite well. After only a few shots, I have learned to correct my high aim. Within thirty seconds I've fired off every round and reloaded. Grossman urges me to try some head shots. This is harder, but again, after an initial error, I can see the holes popping in the head of the silhouette and the sun peeking through.

By now it's clear that whatever else about his theories I might question, Grossman's right about one thing: The .22-caliber pistol is remarkably similar in feel to an arcade gun—the kick is miniscule and it's only slightly heavier. In fact, arcade guns have a heavy cord dangling from them, so after hours of playing, you feel an added weight. You tend to develop muscles that can clearly hold a .22 quite steady.

Learning to Do That

We decide to take things up a notch. "Now," Grossman says, "I want you to try something with a bit more kick to it." He hands me a much bigger gun—his .45-caliber Springfield pistol, the weapon carried by the FBI. A .22 is a potentially lethal gun, as Michael Carneal proved, but ultimately it's pretty lightweight stuff. A .45, however, can really mess someone up.

Including me. The first shot shocks me with the power of its kick and the bullet flies harmlessly over the top of the target. I swallow deeply. My hands are shaking badly. Far more than the .22, this gun is very, very real, and nothing like an arcade toy. The way it kicks around, it's like it has a mind of its own.

Still, what happens next is revealing. Despite my nervousness, I automatically compensate for my panic. Even as my hands tremble, even as I sweat under the gaze of the cops, even as my mind races, my aim instantly improves. Some subconscious part of my brain takes over, and by the second shot I'm again hitting perfectly in the chest area. Shot after shot rips through the target, and I realize in a flash that this is what training is supposed to do—allow you to perform well even under great stress, or when your mind is occupied with other details. Some form of Skinner's operant conditioning, it seems, is in effect.

Then the hammer clicks on the empty chamber. The last shot has been fired. I hand the gun back to Grossman, and he races off to examine my targets.

According to Grossman, the accuracy of neophyte soldiers in training is relatively low. After one week of pistol training, fifty percent of recruits can hit the man-shaped silhouette "with some regularity," and one-quarter can concentrate their shots in the central chest area. Only five percent can place their shots in a small, silver-dollar-sized area. I've checked these stats with other police trainers; they agree the estimates are sound.

As for me? Grossman brings my targets. The shots are all in the center-chest area, the "9" and "10" scoring rings. It's unsettling, yet riveting to look at these close up. The bullet holes are clustered in what seems to be a shockingly tight radius. If this were a real person, hell, I'd have blown their torso to shreds with the first few shots alone.

Grossman seems thrilled. "I would say it was head-and-shoulders above the average first-time shooter." I'm not on par with the best he's seen he says, but I'm shooting as well as a trainee would at the end of a week of training—a week. He gestures to the target. "That would be an A. You're scholarship material. You were rocking and rolling!"

Now comes the inevitable question. Grossman grins at me. "To shoot like you did with that .45 is truly extraordinary. And you've never fired a gun before. Where did you learn to do that?"

A Complex Debate

On the flight back from Mississippi, my shooting targets crammed into a garment bag, I replay the experience in my head—what it means, what it doesn't. I'm still relatively unsettled by my aptitude with deadly force, and impressed by how well Grossman's theory has played out. But I'm also disappointed. On some level, I realize, I didn't want to prove him even partially right. Too frequently, critics assume all gamers are sociopathic freaks. I hardly wanted to push that stereotype further.

But even if Grossman's idea about gun training is correct, it still can't explain what's going on in American high schools-specifically, the motivations of the killers. Hand-eye coordination is one thing; seething rage is quite another. Sure, kids may be able to go on mass rampages, but why would they want to?

Investigators studying the Columbine shooting admitted this fall that they were still baffled by what motivated Dylan Klebold and Eric Harris. "I've been working on this nonstop daily since April 20th and I can't tell you why it happened," lead investigator Kate Battan told Salon magazine. The killers' hatred, it seems, was freefloating in the traditional manner of persecuted teens. Jocks, gays, other nerds, popular kids, minorities, racists—everyone was up for grabs. None of this would shock anyone who went through an even mildly bad adolescence—they know that high school is, socially and psychologically, a shark tank, pitting clique against clique. In that context, it's hard to finger House of the Dead as a singular cause of teen angst. On the contrary, teensploitation TV fare like Manchester Prep or Popular—with their phalanxes of glossy, milk-fed socialites and ugly, brainy losers—is probably more likely to blur your sense of reality. And though largely devoid of physical violence, shows like that are quite capable of training you in the art of teen psychological warfare, a battle in which no gun license is necessary.

Guns themselves, of course, are another obvious issue in recent shootings—and another wrinkle that makes Grossman's theory seem overly pat. Videogame guns don't kill people; real ones do. Yet Grossman, a soldier who wholeheartedly supports the NRA, isn't out there fighting for enhanced gun-control laws. Rather, he thinks current laws are adequate. He also claims kids' access to guns hasn't increased, so guns can't solely be responsible for the rise in shootings. "I grew up with a twelve-gauge shotgun in my bedroom," he notes.

Perhaps most damaging to Grossman's case, however, are academic videogame researchers, some of whom say he has no science to back up his theories. A recent survey by media think-tank Mediascope found that only sixteen studies exist that probe the relationship between videogames and aggression, and their results are mixed. Even if every study agreed that games are homicidal in their impact, sixteen studies is a scientifically insignificant number, say the scientists. It doesn't yet prove anything.

Jeanne Funk, author of several videogame studies and a respected psychologist from the University of Toledo, sighs when I mention Grossman's name. She admires *On Killing*, but thinks his videogame theories have no serious scientific foundation. "He says things have been proven when they haven't," she says. "The fact is, we're just beginning to examine this issue. We don't know. The data are so thin." In pushing his ideas, Grossman relies instead on the thousands of studies that successfully link violent TV shows with aggression, and on the military's experience using simulators. But neither, Funk argues, are easily applicable to gaming. Videogames could have benevolent effects; on the other hand, that could be far, far worse than Grossman's worst nightmares. "But we have nothing to go on right now," she insists.

This, ultimately, is the most frustrating part of the issue. Surrounded by all the firing guns, panicked parents and the media frenzy, simple answers are more seductive than further debate. But every time I'm tempted to dismiss Grossman, I open my closet and pull out those silhouette targets. I check out the cluster of holes in the chest. I remember the jolt of the .45.

Violent Entertainment Should Not Be Marketed to Children

President Bill Clinton

*In the following speech, President Bill Clinton expresses his opin-
ion about violent entertainment: it should not be marketed to
children. He believes that the government should exert pressure
on the entertainment industry to convey this message.*

*President Clinton's speech comes in the aftermath of the
shooting at Columbine High School in Littleton, Colorado, in
which two teenagers shot and killed twelve students and wounded
twenty-four others before taking their own lives. Among the
ramifications of the tragedy was a cultural debate about certain
violent lyrics and movies believed to have influenced the shooters. It is in this context that President Clinton makes his recom-
mendation that the Justice Department and Federal Trade Commission investigate entertainment industry regulations. Clinton
insists that the "cultural assault" of violence in the media can be
mitigated in part by audience-appropriate advertising.*

*Clinton served as President of the United States from 1992 to
2000. Upon leaving office, he founded the William J. Clinton
Foundation to address international causes such as HIV/AIDS
and global warming.*

I thank the Attorney General and Chairman Pitofsky for
their remarks and their commitment. I thank Mayor Corra-
dini, Mayor Kaine, County Executive Curry, and County Executive Dutch Ruppersberger for the interest that our local
government leaders have. I thank Representative Sheila Jack-
son Lee for her passionate commitment to this issue. And all
of you, welcome to the White House.

President Bill Clinton, "Remarks Announcing a Study on Youth Violence and Media
Marketing [Transcript]," *Weekly Compilation of Presidential Documents*, vol. 35, June 7,
1999, pp. 1009–1011. Copyright © 1999 U.S. Government Printing Office.

And most of all, I want to say again how much I appreciate Arthur Sawe for coming here, and for sharing a child's perspective. We have other children in this audience today, and we are really here about them and their future.

Preventing Youth Violence

As Hillary [former first lady, Hillary Clinton] said, the tragedy Littleton had a profound effect on America. It certainly had a profound effect on us and on our family, particularly after we had the chance to go to Colorado and visit with the families of the children who were killed and many of the young children who are still grievously wounded and the kids at the school with them, who are hurting still, and the teachers.

I do think that what Hillary said is right: We sense a determination, not only in that community but throughout our country, not just to grieve about this but to do something about it. The national grassroots campaign against violence against children is rooted in our faith that we can do better.

We know we can prevent more youth violence if we work together, across all the lines that divide us. We know we can do it if we're all willing to assume responsibility and stop trying to assign blame. Of course, the responsibility begins at home. It must be reinforced and supported at schools and houses of worship in the community as a whole. Those of us in public service must also do our part. There is broad and growing consensus for us to do more.

Let me say I am also very grateful that the gun manufacturers came here last month and voiced their support for commonsense restrictions to make it more difficult for guns to get into the hands of children and criminals. I'm encouraged that the Senate acted to close the deadly gun show loophole, to require safety locks to be sold with every handgun, to ban the importation of large-capacity ammunition clips, and ban violent juveniles from owning guns as adults. I hope the House of Representatives will pass these commonsense measures as soon as they return from the Memorial Day recess. We have a lot to do this year, but this should be put at the top of the agenda and not put on hold.

As you have already heard, members of the entertainment industry must also do their part. They and the rest of us cannot kid ourselves. Our children are being fed a dependable daily dose of violence, and it sells. Now, 30 years of studies have shown that this desensitizes our children to violence and to the consequences of it.

Cultural Assault

We now know that by the time the typical American child reaches the age of 18, he or she has seen 200,000 dramatized acts of violence and 40,000 dramatized murders. Kids become attracted to it and more numb to its consequences. As their exposure to violence grows, so, in some deeply troubling cases of particularly vulnerable children, does the taste for it. We should not be surprised that half the video games a typical seventh grader plays are violent.

Anyone who doubts the impact of the cultural assault can look at what now, over 30 years, amounts to somewhere over 300 studies, all of whom show that there is a link between sustained exposure, hour after hour, day after day, week after week, year after year, to violent entertainment and violent behavior.

What the studies say, quite simply, is that the boundary between fantasy and reality violence, which is a clear line for most adults, can become very blurred for vulnerable children. Kids steeped in the culture of violence do become desensitized to it and more capable of committing it themselves.

That is why I have strongly urged people in the entertainment industry to consider the consequences of what they create and how they advertise it. One can value the first amendment right to free speech and at the same time care for and act with restraint. Our administration has worked to give parents more tools to protect their kids, to block violent programming from entering their living room with the V-chip and the rating system. We've made progress on parental screening for Internet and ratings for Internet game sites.

Still, when violent entertainment made for adults is marketed to children, it undermines the rating system designed to protect them. And if you look at some of these ads, it's hard to argue with a straight face that the games were made for adults in the first place, like the one Arthur mentioned.

The Role of Advertising

Advertisements have a particular role here. They have the power to egg children on and lure them in. Every parent knows what response a commercial for sugar cereal or the latest "Star Wars" toy will get from their children. People advertise because it works. They want that product, and one way or the other, they're determined to get it. So we ought to think twice about the impact of ads for so-called "first-person shooter video games," like the recent ad for a game that invites players to, and I quote, "Get in touch with your gun-toting, cold-blooded murdering side."

I was given—today Arthur brought me the magazine with the ad that he mentioned, and he was kind enough to mark it for me. There really is a gun here. It says, "More fun than shooting your neighbor's cat." I was given another ad that says, "What kind of psycho drives a school bus into a war zone?" And here's a school bus, heavily armed. This came out right after the incident in Springfield, Oregon.

Here's an ad that turns the argument I just made on its head: "Psychiatrists say it's important to feel something when you kill." And then it goes on to say, "You ought to get this technology because it bumps, and you feel it." It says, "Every sensation, every vibration, every mutilation, nine programmable weapons buttons. Customizable feedback software. Push the stick that pushes back, and feel your pain." And here's one that's the most unbelievable of all. It says, "Kill your friends guilt-free."

Now, obviously, Arthur has the inner strength and the good upbringing to reject that kind of violent appeal. Most of our children do, but not all of our children do. We cannot be surprised when this kind of thing has an impact on our most vulnerable children. Is it 100 percent to blame? No. It's easier to get guns in this society. Parents on average spend 29 hours a week less with their children than they did 30 years ago because of the demands of work and commuting, the busyness of daily life.

But when you put it all together, there are bound to be explosive negative consequences. That's why today I am asking the Department of Justice and the Federal Trade Commission to study the extent to which the video game, music, and movie markets do actually market violence to children, and whether those industries are abiding by their own voluntary systems of regulations.

Society's Most Important Job

To any company that sells violent products, I say, children are more than consumers. I understand nobody made anybody buy any of this stuff. But every day, a responsible society declines to do some things for short-term gain that it can do. And that is what we have to think about. These children are our future, our most precious resource. Raising them is any society's most important job.

Don't make young people want what your own rating systems say they shouldn't have. I might say again, as has already been acknowledged, many, many people in the entertainment industry have worked with us on this, on the ratings system, on the V-chip, on the screening technology for the Internet.

I noticed one network executive, a few days ago, actually canceled a program because its violent content was inappropriate, and I applaud that. But I also read with concern the news that some of the new programming coming up for this fall on some networks will be even more violent than last year's. The time has come to show some restraint, even if it has a short-term impact on the bottom line.

I also want to challenge the owners of movie theaters and video stores, distributors, anyone at any point of sale, enforce the rating systems on the products that you sell. Check the IDs. Draw the line. If underage children are buying violent video games or getting into R-rated movies, the rating system should be enforced to put a stop to it. And if, as many of us suspect, there is still too much gratuitous violence in PG-13-rated movies, the rating systems themselves should be reevaluated.

We Can Do Something

I want to thank Senators Brownback, Lieberman, Hatch, and Kohl for the bipartisan work they have done on this issue. Again, I want to commend State Representative Mary Lou Dickerson from Washington, who read about young Arthur, helped to create a task force on video game violence; and thanks to her work with . . . the Mothers Against Violence in America and the Washington Retailers' Association, who are all represented here today, video game retailers in Washington State now voluntarily sign a pledge to parents, committing themselves to check IDs and block sales of violent games to minors. That's something that ought to happen in every State in the United States of America.

Again I say, we can do something about this. It will take a grassroots campaign. It will take everybody doing his or her part. This is a problem we face together, a problem America can solve together. There is no more urgent task for our future.

You were all looking at this young man speaking today, thinking, what a wonderful thing that a person that young could speak so clearly, so confidently, about things that are so right. You look around at the other young people here today who are involved in this effort in some way or another, and you thank God that we have this legacy of children.

A lot of those kids that haven't made it through all these school violence incidents were just as good, just as fine, had just as much to give the world. We've got to quit fooling around with this. We've got a chance. Our hearts are open. Our ears are open. Our heads are thinking.

I know this stuff sells. But that doesn't make it right.

Thank you, and God bless you.

Violence in Entertainment Media is Good for Kids

Gerard Jones

In the following selection, Gerard Jones writes favorably of violence in entertainment media. He maintains that the intertwining of violence and fantasy in the form of movies, television, comic books, videogames, and music can have a positive influence on children. This sort of creative violence, as he terms it, can serve to empower children because it is a tool through which they can master self-control and fear.

Although Jones acknowledges that violent media can occasionally have harmful effects, he disagrees with those who say children must be shielded from it altogether. He insists that for every one person exposure to media violence has hurt, there are many more people whom it has helped.

Jones is a comic book author with a number of credits, including Marvel Comics and DC Comics. He is also the author of three books offering commentary on pop culture.

At 13 I was alone and afraid. Taught by my well-meaning, progressive, English-teacher parents that violence was wrong, that rage was something to be overcome and cooperation was always better than conflict, I suffocated my deepest fears and desires under a nice-boy persona. Placed in a small, experimental school that was wrong for me, afraid to join my peers in their bumptious rush into adolescent boyhood, I withdrew into passivity and loneliness. My parents, not trusting the violent world of the late 1960s, built a wall between me and the crudest elements of American pop culture.

Then the Incredible Hulk smashed through it.

Gerard Jones, "Violent Media Is Good for Kids," *Mother Jones.* www.motherjones.com. Copyright © 2000 Foundation for National Progress. Reproduced by permission.

Violence and Fantasy

One of my mother's students convinced her that Marvel Comics, despite their apparent juvenility and violence, were in fact devoted to lofty messages of pacifism and tolerance. My mother borrowed some, thinking they'd be good for me. And so they were. But not because they preached lofty messages of benevolence. They were good for me because they were juvenile. And violent.

The character who caught me, and freed me, was the Hulk: overgendered and undersocialized, half-naked and half-witted, raging against a frightened world that misunderstood and persecuted him. Suddenly I had a fantasy self to carry my stifled rage and buried desire for power. I had a fantasy self who was a self: unafraid of his desires and the world's disapproval, unhesitating and effective in action. "Puny boy follow Hulk!" roared my fantasy self, and I followed.

I followed him to new friends—other sensitive geeks chasing their own inner brutes—and I followed him to the arrogant, self-exposing, self-assertive, superheroic decision to become a writer. Eventually, I left him behind, followed more sophisticated heroes, and finally my own lead along a twisting path to a career and an identity. In my 30s, I found myself writing action movies and comic books. I wrote some Hulk stories, and met the geek-geniuses who created him. I saw my own creations turned into action figures, cartoons, and computer games. I talked to the kids who read my stories. Across generations, genders, and ethnicities I kept seeing the same story: people pulling themselves out of emotional traps by immersing themselves in violent stories. People integrating the scariest, most fervently denied fragments of their psyches into fuller senses of selfhood through fantasies of superhuman combat and destruction.

I have watched my son living the same story—transforming himself into a bloodthirsty dinosaur to embolden himself for the plunge into preschool, a Power Ranger to muscle through a social competition in kindergarten. In the first grade, his friends started climbing a tree at school. But he was afraid: of falling, of the centipedes crawling on the trunk, of sharp branches, of his friends' derision. I took my cue from his own fantasies and read him old Tarzan comics, rich in combat and bright with flashing knives. For two weeks he lived in them. Then he put them aside. And he climbed the tree.

But all the while, especially in the wake of the recent burst of school shootings, I heard pop psychologists insisting that violent stories are harmful to kids, heard teachers begging parents to keep their kids away from "junk culture," heard a guilt-stricken friend with a son who loved Pokémon lament, "I've turned into the bad mom who lets her kid eat sugary cereal and watch cartoons!"

That's when I started the research.

Creative Violence Is Empowering

"Fear, greed, power-hunger, rage: these are aspects of our selves that we try not to experience in our lives but often want, even need, to experience vicariously through stories of others," writes Melanie Moore, Ph.D., a psychologist who works with urban teens. "Children need violent entertainment in order to explore the inescapable feelings that they've been taught to deny, and to reintegrate those feelings into a more whole, more complex, more resilient selfhood."

Moore consults to public schools and local governments, and is also raising a daughter. For the past three years she and I have been studying the ways in which children use violent stories to meet their emotional and developmental needs— and the ways in which adults can help them use those stories healthily. With her help I developed Power Play, a program for helping young people improve their self-knowledge and sense of potency through heroic, combative storytelling.

We've found that every aspect of even the trashiest pop-culture story can have its own developmental function. Pretending to have superhuman powers helps children conquer the feelings of powerlessness that inevitably come with being so young and small. The dual-identity concept at the heart of many superhero stories helps kids negotiate the conflicts between the inner self and the public self as they work through the early stages of socialization. Identification with a rebellious, even destructive, hero helps children learn to push back against a modern culture that cultivates fear and teaches dependency.

At its most fundamental level, what we call "creative violence"—head-bonking cartoons, bloody videogames, playground karate, toy guns—gives children a tool to master their rage. Children will feel rage. Even the sweetest and most civilized of them, even those whose parents read the better class of literary magazines, will feel rage. The world is uncontrollable and incomprehensible; mastering it is a terrifying, enraging task. Rage can be an energizing emotion, a shot of courage to push us to resist greater threats, take more control, than we ever thought we could. But rage is also the emotion our culture distrusts the most. Most of us are taught early on to fear our own. Through immersion in imaginary combat and identification with a violent protagonist, children engage the rage they've stifled, come to fear it less, and become more capable of utilizing it against life's challenges.

Violent Media Helps More Than Hurts

I knew one little girl who went around exploding with fantasies so violent that other moms would draw her mother aside to whisper, "I think you should know something about Emily . . . ." Her parents were separating, and she was small, an only child, a tomboy at an age when her classmates were dividing sharply along gender lines. On the playground she acted out "Sailor Moon" fights, and in the classroom she wrote stories about people being stabbed with knives. The more adults tried to control her stories, the more she acted out the roles of her angry heroes: breaking rules, testing limits, roaring threats.

Then her mother and I started helping her tell her stories. She wrote them, performed them, drew them like comics: sometimes bloody, sometimes tender, always blending the images of pop culture with her own most private fantasies. She came out of it just as fiery and strong, but more self-controlled and socially competent: a leader among her peers, the one student in her class who could truly pull boys and girls together.

I worked with an older girl, a middle-class "nice girl," who held herself together through a chaotic family situation and a tumultuous adolescence with gangsta rap. In the mythologized street violence of Ice T, the rage and strutting of his music and lyrics, she found a theater of the mind in which she could be powerful, ruthless, invulnerable. She avoided the heavy drug use that sank many of her peers, and flowered in college as a writer and political activist.

I'm not going to argue that violent entertainment is harmless. I think it has helped inspire some people to real-life violence. I am going to argue that it's helped hundreds of people for every one it's hurt, and that it can help far more if we learn to use it well. I am going to argue that our fear of "youth violence" isn't well-founded on reality, and that the fear can do more harm than the reality. We act as though our highest priority is to prevent our children from growing up into murderous thugs—but modern kids are far more likely to grow up too passive, too distrustful of themselves, too easily manipulated.

We send the message to our children in a hundred ways that their craving for imaginary gun battles and symbolic killings is wrong, or at least dangerous. Even when we don't call for censorship or forbid "Mortal Kombat," we moan to other parents within our kids' earshot about the "awful violence" in the entertainment they love. We tell our kids that it isn't nice to play-fight, or we steer them from some monstrous action figure to a pro-social doll. Even in the most progressive households, where we make such a point of letting children feel what they feel, we rush to substitute an enlightened discussion for the raw material of rageful fantasy. In the process, we risk confusing them about their natural aggression in the same way the Victorians confused their children about their sexuality. When we try to protect our children from their own feelings and fantasies, we shelter them not against violence but against power and selfhood.

Moral Relativism, Not Violence, Is the Problem

Jonah Goldberg

*In this article, Jonah Goldberg views the debate on media vio-
lence through a political lens. He contends that the issue of violence in entertainment media arises every four years as presidential campaigns ensue. Goldberg then delineates the dialogue
about the media violence issue as expressed by both ends of the
political spectrum.*

*Goldberg offers a critique of Hollywood as well as of the de-
bate on violence in the media itself. He contends that the political denunciations are out of focus: It is moral relativism and im-
morality in films, not the violence, that render the most harmful
effect on viewers. He believes that there is not a substantial
enough correlation between crime rates and the distribution of
violent movies to place the blame solely on violence. Goldberg is
critical of the trend in films and television that tends to celebrate
characters who reject the moral order. In his view, this is ultimately a dangerous premise because the idea of no absolute right
or wrong means that perpetrators of violence can become heroes.
It is in this context that violence in the media has its most cul-
turally damaging results.*

Goldberg is editor-at-large and columnist for National Review Online. *He is also a political commentator who has made
numerous appearances on radio and TV talk shows.*

L ike presidential elections and the Olympics, political denunciations of Hollywood violence have become a bed-
rock quadrennial American tradition. At least every four
years—sometimes more often, if there's a school shooting—

Jonah Goldberg, "Violent Fantasy: It's Not the Hollywood Gore That's the Problem,"
National Review, vol. 52, October 23, 2000. Copyright © 2000 by National Review, Inc.,
215 Lexington Avenue, New York, NY 10016. Reproduced by permission.

movie-industry lobbyist Jack Velenti simultaneously sucks up to politicians and lectures them about the First Amendment. Liberal activists who denounce Joe Camel as a pied piper of social coercion swear that screen idols have no influence on human behavior. Television executives who make billions of dollars off the persuasive power of 30-second commercials declare that the 26- and 54-minute programs those ads punctuate have no net impact on their viewers.

The Message of Moral Relativism

It shouldn't surprise anyone that there are no new arguments since the last go-around, when [U.S. Senator] Bob Dole denounced "nightmares of depravity" and the "mainstreaming of deviancy" in a slew of films he'd never seen. This season, a Federal Trade Commission report—released with precise political timing—details how the film industry targets very young audiences for mature films. While this gives the controversy a newsier feel, the report's details merely confirm what everybody knew: Hollywood makes its money from kids.

Of course, what really makes this year's repeat of history a farce is that this time it is the Democrats who are bemoaning the "coarsening of our culture." In years past, we could at least expect some ritualistic huffing and puffing about free speech from the Hollywood liberals; but this time around they know that their Al [Gore] doesn't really mean it. "Go, go, go, Al! We need a little spanking!" cheered Bette Midler at a star-studded fundraiser recently, giving full expression to the gravity with which Hollywood views this "crisis."

Despite all of the posturing, nobody is addressing the real problem with Hollywood: It's not the violence at all, but the message of moral relativism. Violence has been a constant in world culture. You can draw a line starting from cave paintings, and trace it through all visual media up to this weekend's latest blockbuster. Greek tragedies, Shakespeare's plays, Japanese picture books, and Native American oral histories can hold their own with just about any Schwarzenegger film in terms of murder and gore. Talking about violence—even graphic violence—as something "new" is like talking about a disturbing rise in the use of percussion instruments in music.

The antiviolence handwringers contend that it is the graphic, realistic nature of modern depictions that does real damage. But if simple film violence were the problem, one would look for some correlation between crime rates and violent-movie distribution. Such correlations remain elusive.

The Problem of Context

A more realistic contention is that while movie violence is not bad in itself, it can be bad when presented in a morally harmful context. During the 1992–93 round of Hollywood-bashing, Sen. Paul Simon threatened the television networks with government "action" if they didn't clean themselves up; in response, the networks sponsored a UCLA study that concluded that "context is the key to the determination of whether or not the use of violence is appropriate." The problem for liberals, though, is that they don't think there are many contexts where violence is permissible-save, perhaps, in cautionary tales about Nazis, southern slaveowners, and military homophobes. The Left always despised Dirty Harry movies, for example, because the moral context of those films suggested that criminals were, in fact, criminals, and that a liberal do-gooder court system was allowing the bad guys to rule the streets.

In a 1992 article in *Reason* magazine, aptly entitled "Faster, Hollywood, Kill! Kill" Tevi Troy suggested that the popularity of *Dirty Harry, Death Wish*, and other violent vigilante films was actually a healthy expression of public discontent with the crime wave of the 1960s and '70s. Watching Dirty Harry administer rough justice was a healthy release valve for frustrated Americans who did not, after all, take the law into their own hands upon leaving the theater. When Dirty Harry killed, he may have been defying the legal order—but he was still confirming the moral order. Troy's analysis is surely correct: Action heroes from Perseus to Captain Kirk have always taken the law into their own hands; they are men of action, with a well-defined sense of the moral right.

This was the central appeal of the films of John Wayne, who—from 1949 to 1974—was on the annual list of Top 10 biggest box-office movie stars for a record 25 years. Out of his well over 100 films, you can count on two hands the number that didn't depict him shooting, slugging, or ordering the shooting or slugging of someone. A whole generation of men wanted to imitate Wayne, seeing him as the definition of an authentic male. The Left criticized his films for glorifying war, because they didn't show the terrible consequences of battle; as a result, in many of the Left-influenced war films of the last 30 years, we have seen in much more graphic detail how unpleasant and messy killing can be.

A Complicated History

Violence in popular entertainment, then, has a complicated history; it's neither new nor especially harmful. What really is new and harmful is the trendy moral relativism that characterizes so many movies and TV shows. These cultural products receive rave reviews from liberal activists for their "positive" (and relatively nonviolent) content. But in these films, protagonists do not defy the legal order so that they can uphold a higher moral order; instead, these "heroes" rebel against the notion that there is any moral order at all. . . .

. . . *American Beauty* won the Oscar for best picture last year [1999], but it wasn't alone in its message. Indeed, the winners in almost every major category involved some variation on the theme that external morel authority is illegitimate, or that personally designed morality is superior. For example, another academy favorite was *Boys Don't Cry*, a film about a petty criminal, a transsexual woman who prefers masquerading as a boy in order to seduce and bed teenage girls. What raised the film to heroic status for Hollywood is its assertion that America remains, at heart, a nation of sexual fascists who cruelly impose conventional bourgeois standards on courageous nonconformists.

The entertainment industry has hammered home the idea that conformity of any kind is a sign of spiritual surrender. While films with excessive violence often receive considerable critical and popular scrutiny, the idea that we are all our own priests is celebrated throughout the popular culture. This idea is found even in technically well-made films like *Dead Poets Society* and the pernicious *Pleasantville*, both of which redefined the concept of "to thine own self be true" to mean "thine own self is the only truth." It is also the moral of hundreds of individual TV shows and movies; it is the core social and political insight of rock 'n' roll and rap music. How else to explain the familiar litany of rap songs which exult in killing and rape?

This attitude makes violent films all the more poisonous. In a world where no set of moral principles is superior to any other, why not make heroes out of murderers? This is the lesson of nearly the entire Quentin Tarantino oeuvre and its many ripoffs. More and more often, we are seeing psychopaths and serial killers as protagonists. An early example can be found in the 1984 *Terminator*, in which the audience is invited to see things through the eyes of a killing machine—and enjoy it. Since then, the pace has only accelerated. In the 1991 *Silence of the Lambs*, Hannibal Lecter was a profoundly sympathetic cannibalistic serial killer; in the upcoming sequel, if it's adapted loyally from the novel—he will be the hero.

An Amoral Worldview

What's important to remember about this amoral context for violence is that it stems from the amoral worldview of the Hollywood filmmakers; and at the very core of that worldview is sex. It's a bit of cliche by now to point out that liberals fret over violence in movies, and conservatives about sex. But there's a good reason for that. We know from endless studies as well as common sense end experience that a tendency for violence, especially in boys, manifests itself without much prodding from the culture. Give a young boy a Barbie doll and he will, in all likelihood, try to make a gun out of it. But sex is more complicated. Young boys who know a million ways to kill a man—hypothetically—are quite ignorant about sex, if left to their own devices until puberty.

Hollywood changes that dynamic. In its contention that not only should sexual appetites be indulged, but those who most fully indulge them, without regret or remorse, are living the most authentic lives, it offers young boys a recipe for mayhem. . . .

Its [This idea's] central insight is that the moral concerns of others, even the worth of others, can be dismissed. The FTC report that launched this latest round of Hollywood-bashing was itself prompted by the Columbine massacre in Littleton, Colo. But children in Colorado have had access to guns and been exposed to violence for over a century. What nobody ever told those kids until recently is that you can buy your own morality retail.

Media Violence Often Has No Moral Lesson

Patrick McCormick

This article by Patrick McCormick approaches the issue of media violence from the perspective of consequences. Unlike psychologists and physicians who weigh in on the issue, he does not emphasize the psychological effects of viewing violence. Instead, Mc-Cormick criticizes the entertainment industry's tendency to overlook the transformative effects of violence on the victims and perpetrators depicted. He believes that in films and television violence is shown readily but its effects those involved are not.

To illustrate his case, McCormick discusses several films in recent years that supplement violence by exploring the related themes of retribution and redemption. He suggest that it is when the lingering effects of violence are avoided or minimized that violence in entertainment media truly becomes problematic. Violence has consequences, he maintains, and they should be understood. McCormick also augments his viewpoint with a brief digression into violence in war and its effects on those who experienced or witnessed it.

McCormick is Professor of Christian Ethics at Gonzaga University, where he is Chair of the Religious Studies Department. He has published a number or articles on Christian ethics and Catholic social thought.

Many complain that TV and movie violence has become commonplace and coarse, but what I worry about is that too much of it has no cost or consequence. If we are going to watch people beating, torturing, and killing other human beings, it should be disturbing and frightening. We ought to flinch. And realistic violence should wreak havoc in the lives of those it touches.

Patrick McCormick, "The Walking Wounder," *U.S. Catholic*, January 2006, pp. 42–43. Copyright © 2006 by Claretian Publications. Reproduced by permission.

Consequences

But heroes in most action shows are unscathed by the violence they employ, and audiences care little about the long-term effects of this mayhem on victims and families. Television and movie cops abuse suspects without repercussion, litter the highways with crashed and burning cars without civilian casualties, and throw down in countless shoot-outs without suffering trauma, nightmares, or depression. And when the shooting and bombing is done, no audience lingers to watch victims and their families grapple with their shattered lives.

A few recent films track violence's devastating wake. In Todd Field's *In the Bedroom* (Miramax) we watch a 30-year year marriage shipwrecked by the murder of a couple's son. Christopher Nolan's *Memento* (Columbia Tristar) shows us a grieving husband traumatized and corrupted by the violence that took his wife. And Nolan's noir thriller *Insomnia* (Warner Brothers) gives us a policeman hounded and haunted by the consequences of his own violence.

Violence casts a long shadow in Brad Anderson's psychological thriller *The Machinist* (Filmax), for which Christian Bale dropped 60 pounds to play a factory worker being eaten alive by an undigested piece of his past. It has been a year since Trevor Resnik (Bale) had a good night's sleep or a solid meal, and the depressed and increasingly paranoid machinist cannot figure out why he is slowly turning into a walking cadaver, or why people no one else sees harass him and leave him mysteriously threatening notes.

But Resnik, who has suppressed the memory of a violent act he committed, will continue to be haunted by a phantom pain that has him night-crawling cafés and chatting up people who aren't there anymore until he acknowledges his guilt and faces the consequences of his violence. Then, at long last, his unconscious will stop carving the mark of Cain in his flesh and allow him a good night's rest.

An American Myth

You wouldn't know it to look at him, but café owner and small-town dad Tom Stall (Viggo Mortensen) also has *A History of Violence* (New Line Cinema) in David Cronenberg's tale about a killer who tries to escape his past by creating his own witness protection program. For two decades Tom—or Joey as his buddies from the old neighborhood like to call him—manages to hide out among the quiet townsfolk of a sleepy Indiana burg, only to be unmasked when he commits a violent act of heroism that evokes cheers from his neighbors and catches the attention of old friends interested in settling accounts.

In Cronenberg's film Tom's heroic act uncovers a killer who finds he cannot forget or outrun his past and unleashes forces and consequences set in motion long ago by Joey's own violence—forces that endanger, traumatize, and corrupt Tom's wife and children, and could well destroy his family.

But *A History of Violence* also unmasks the audience cheering 'Tom on as he slaughters a platoon of movie villains. Each time our hero/villain swings into action we are less certain of his motives and less confident in the redemptive power of violence, a core American myth. Even if Joey kills all the bad guys, what will that do to his family and children, and how will he and they ever find a peaceful life again? Perhaps violence is not the solution to life's most intractable problems. Perhaps it *is* one of life's most intractable problems.

Soldiers and PTSD

These tales of men trying to suppress the memory of their violence and return to normal life seem particularly poignant in the wake of reports about the rising incidence of post-traumatic stress disorder among soldiers returning from Afghanistan and Iraq.

In October the *Wall Street Journal* reported that a highly-decorated Army Ranger captain honored by President Bush in his 2003 State of the Union address has quietly resigned from the army after being diagnosed with severe symptoms of PTSD. Studies in *The New England Journal of Medicine* and elsewhere suggest that 17 percent of the 360,000 troops brought back from Iraq and Afghanistan may suffer from this condition, and the Veterans Administration has already diagnosed nearly 10,000 veterans as having PTSD.

Experts believe soldiers underreport mental and emotional wounds for fear of being considered cowards or malingerers and suggest that the incidence of PTSD could rise in the months and years ahead. Most agree the military and Veterans Administration are not equipped to support all these wounded soldiers.

The Whole Story

In *The Things They Carried*, Pulitzer Prize-winning novelist and Vietnam veteran Tim O'Brien warned about war stories that hide the obscenity of violence, that make violence seem heroic and attractive to the young men and women sucked into its maw. In other works he tracked the lingering effects of war on returning veterans. But the wounded soldiers who return from war are just the tip of the iceberg. Ninety percent of the casualties of modern warfare are civilians, and the effects of war linger for generations. Land mines left behind from previous wars continue to kill more people across the planet than any other weapon of mass destruction, and the infrastructure destroyed by bombs and sanctions took a million lives in Iraq in the decade after the first Gulf War.

Our violent entertainments need to tell the whole story, to track the long and tortured history of violence, the way it bends back on its perpetrators, the unfolding carnage it leaves in its spreading wake. The problem with violent stories is not that they are too gory, but that they are not gruesome enough.

THE
HISTORY
OF
ISSUES

CHAPTER 4

Proposed Solutions to Media Violence Issues

Chapter Preface

The multitude of perspectives on the media violence debate has resulted in a myriad of ideas as to how to address it politically, legally, and socially. Yet because of the lack of consensus that characterizes the issue, many proposed political and legal solutions have not obtained the support necessary to make fundamental changes in those realms. Divided interpretations concerning First Amendment-endowed free speech rights are the primary reasons for the stumbling blocks: some believe the government should step in and others maintain that the entertainment industry should self-regulate.

Addressing media violence, therefore, remains primarily under the domain of grass-roots organizations. Such groups advocate action on a societal level as a foundation for larger-scale change. Thus, media violence has prompted the formation of media literacy groups whose mission is to make health practitioners, teachers, and parents, and children well-informed.

As a social movement, opposition to media violence underscores the need for research and education. This approach to the issue attempts to avoid the finger-pointing that has plagued media violence over the course of its history. Promoting awareness enables individuals to make informed decisions. Health care professionals and teachers can talk to parents about the research of media violence effects and make recommendations, parents can monitor what their children should and should not watch (or play) and how to place media violence in context, and children can equip themselves with frameworks for analysis that will help them understand and interpret violence in the media. The rationale is that taken together, such steps can mitigate the societal effects of violence in the media, whether those effects are universally agreed-upon or not. Ultimately, the groups hope to create a broad enough base of support to facilitate meaningful political and legal change.

Government Regulations on Violence in Entertainment Media

Jess Cagle, Mitch Frank, and Mark Thompson

This article by Jess Cagle, Mitch Frank, and Mark Thompson examines violence in the media in the context of federal regulation. Children are exposed not only to media violence but also to the marketing campaigns designed to promote such media. The authors pose questions as to whether the government should intervene and if so, to what extent it should intervene.

Cagle et al. provide examples of violence in modern American pop culture in the music, television, video game, and film industries. The authors also cite actions taken by Congress and a report generated by the Federal Trade Commission in order to frame their discussion of government involvement in media advertising. The issue arising with government regulation is the First Amendment: some argue that entertainment, violence and all, is protected under the free speech amendment. Others claim that the First Amendment does not guarantee minors the right to buy everything that adults can. The authors suggest that nudging the entertainment industry to self-regulate and self-censor may be the most viable option.

Cagle is assistant managing editor at People *magazine. Frank is a reporter for* Time *magazine and the author of a book about September 11th. Thompson is the national security correspondent for* Time.

Eminem, the white rapper who also operates under the name Slim Shady, is this year's chief specimen of music-industry magic. His new album, the one in which he rhapso-

Jess Cagle, Mitch Frank, and Mark Thompson, "Washington to Hollywood: Oh, Behave: Movies, CDs and Video Games Are Already Playing Rough with Kids. Should Government Elbow In?" *Time*, vol. 156, September 25, 2000, p. 44. Copyright © 2000 Time, Inc. All rights reserved. Reproduced by permission.

dizes about raping his mother, stabbing gays and so forth, has been in the Top 10 since May, with sales in the U.S. of more than 5 million and climbing. Sample line: "Slim Shady does not give a f___ what you think. If you don't like it, you can suck his f___ing c___." Got that, folks?

Questionable Marketing

Most adults are embarrassed to admit anymore that they might find a movie or a song too much to stomach. They are not so complacent about their kids. The rough edges of pop culture scrape harder these days, and its most extravagant enchantments are promoted to ever younger kids. When your 10-year-old comes home singing "Bitch I'ma kill you"—Eminem again, in a Valentine to his mother—you don't care if you once adored Richard Pryor and William Burroughs. You turn into one of those angry swing voters.

This, naturally, is where the Federal Trade Commission comes in. Last week the FTC released a report on how movie studios, music companies and video-game makers push violent products on children. Landing as it did in the middle of the campaign season, the report caught the attention of Washington at the highest levels of presidential ambition. Al Gore gave the entertainment companies six months to shape up their marketing practices or face unspecified retaliation from Washington. The Senate Commerce Committee, chaired by John McCain, held a hearing to examine the FTC conclusions. Senate colleague Joe Lieberman showed up to express his and Gore's distress. Dick Cheney's wife Lynne, former head of the National Endowment for the Humanities, arrived to cite Eminem as proof that the problem is not just how the entertainment companies sell. "There is a problem with the products," she noted.

The report was requested by Bill Clinton more than a year ago, in the aftermath of the Columbine school massacre, when raw pop culture was blamed for furnishing some of the mental climate in which the killers let their grievances fester. Sidestepping the interminable question of what role song lyrics and movies play in real violence, Clinton asked the FTC just to determine whether the movies, pop music and video games that manufacturers themselves label as questionable for kids were being marketed to kids anyway. The report concluded that "the answer are plainly, yes."

Not An Accident

At the commission's request, internal marketing documents and other evidence were provided by more than 60 companies, including Disney, Fox and Sony as well as Warner Bros. Films and Warner Music Group, both owned by Time Warner. After sifting through those, the FTC decided that the three industries often push violent product in places where young people are a large part of the audience. Though the report did not cite films or studios by name, it did find that R-rated films were advertised in high school newspapers, offered to teens through free preview screenings and advertised on programs watched heavily by children, such as *Xena: Warrior Princess, South Park* and professional wrestling. (Professional wrestling? It would be fair to say the report passed up the chance to observe that some of this "children's" programming is skeevier than anything in R-rated movies.) At the Senate hearings, McCain raised the example of Sony Pictures attempting to place ads on Nickelodeon, a network specifically created for kids, for the skull-blasting Bruce Willis film *The Fifth Element*, which was rated PG-13. Nickelodeon refused the ads.

The FTC also decided that entertainment companies don't just accidentally rein in teens and children; they often target them deliberately in their marketing strategies. The report says an unnamed studio distributed flyers for an R-rated film to youth groups like the Camp Fire Boys and Girls. Video-game makers routinely identified kids under 17 as a big catch in media strategies for games rated M, for mature buyers. Dale Pollock, dean of the film school at the North Carolina School of the Arts, produced the 1996 film *Set It Off*. It was violent, raw and rated R, but Pollock says its distributor, New Line, marketed it to young audiences. "People are naive to think marketers are scrupulous in trying to avoid exposing R-rated films to [kids]," he says. "The exact opposite is true." New Line, a subsidiary of Time Warner, had no comment.

First Amendment Protection

Advertising adult product to teenagers would make no sense if they couldn't buy it. But the labeling systems for music and video games have no teeth. Some large retailers refuse to sell kids M-rated video games or CDs that carry parental-advisory stickers, but most will. Theater owners are not exactly vigilant about enforcing the film-ratings code—something known to any 14-year-old who ever went to the box office at a multiplex, bought a ticket for a PG film, then strolled into a theater playing a film rated R.

The accused industries complain that the magazines and TV shows they advertise with, the ones that reach some kids, are often the same ones they have to use to reach adults. But on the day after the report was released, Disney announced a package of new policies, including a promise that it would provide in its advertising explanations of why any of its films received PG-13, R or NC-17 rating—for instance, for violence, sex, profanity or drug use—and that its ABC-TV network would no longer accept ads for R-rated movies during prime time before 9 p.m. Jack Valenti, head of the Motion Picture Association of America, admitted to the committee that the FTC report identified some practices—like focus groups for 10-year-olds—that should end. But he insists that the ratings system adopted by the movie industry in 1968 is working as intended. "Eighty-one percent of parents are satisfied with the system," he told TIME, citing an FTC survey. "We must be doing something right."

One day after the FTC issued its report, South Carolina attorney general Charlie Condon called it a "smoking gun" that would allow him and other state attorneys general to sue the entertainment companies in the same way they successfully sued the tobacco industry. "They're going after these kids full bore," he says. "It's like an aspirin company marketing adult aspirin to children in violation of their own standards." But a class action of the kind that brought down the cigarette makers would be a hard case. While the connection between smoking and cancer is backed by solid medical evidence, it would not be so easy to prove in court a connection between Marilyn Manson—last year's Eminem—and social problems like increased violence. And unlike tobacco, those movies, CDs and video games are protected by the First Amendment, which limits the steps that government can take against them.

Intimidated the Entertainment Industry

All the same, the First Amendment does not guarantee minors the right to purchase the same material that adults can. The FTC report suggested that more retailers should not let kids buy stickered CDs and video games, just as teens are barred from NC-17 films. This would allow record labels and video-game makers to release whatever they please, and adults to buy it and even pass it on to their kids if they thought that was O.K. But that's a prospect that makes entertainment executives nervous, since the market for the raunchiest and most belligerent pop culture is made up largely of teenage boys. Deprived of that market, Eminem would have to make the case for himself as an artist among adults, where—who knows?—maybe he could make it. But it would be harder for him to move 5 million units.

John McCain was furious that no studio heads showed up to testify before his committee. They all pleaded scheduling conflicts. So he set a second hearing for next week that the execs are expected to fit into their calendars.

Nobody is suggesting a government body to meddle in popular culture. The real aim here is to intimidate the entertainment companies into reining in themselves, as they did with the bumptious movie-industry Hays office of the 1930s and '40s and the Comics Magazine Association of America, an industry group formed in 1954 after Senate hearings into bloody and smutty comic books. It gave its seal of approval only to comic books that went easy on the cleavage and eye gouging. Most retailers would not sell comics that did not earn the association's seal. The system broke down in the 1970s, but for two decades it kept Batman from drinking blood and Wonder Woman dressed. What the politicians would prefer again is that the entertainment companies hold the line themselves. Of course, in a world where WWF Smackdown! qualifies as children's TV, nobody really knows where that line is supposed to be.

Health Care Professionals Should Factor the News into the Media Violence Debate

Juliette H. Walma van der Molen

Dr. Juliette Walma van der Molen argues, in the following article, that health care professionals should broaden their conception of media violence. She believes that in addition to violence in entertainment media, real-life violent images in the news should be part of the debate.

To support her position, Walma van der Molen refers to recent research concerning the potential negative effects on children of viewing violence (as well as one of its corollaries, suffering) in the news. The studies she discusses address effects such as fear, aggression, and desensitization. She points out that violence in the news incorporates both intended violence (such as war or a crime scene) as well as unintended violence (such as accidents or natural disasters). Walma van der Molen's nuanced definition of violence also includes vandalism and plunder. She concludes with some research suggestions and practical recommendations for health care professionals.

Psychologist Walma van der Molen is Associate Professor in the Amsterdam School of Communications Research at the University of Amsterdam. Among her research interest is studying children's fear reactions to news and entertainment media.

Television news is filled with violence and suffering. Local news, which is widely used by Americans, is often found to overemphasize brutal crime and to rely heavily on sensational presentations of violence. In addition, analyses of the

Juliette H. Walma van der Molen, "Violence and Suffering in Television News: Toward a Broader Conception of Harmful Television Content for Children," *Pediatrics*, vol. 113, 2004, pp. 1771–1775. Copyright © 2004 American Academy of Pediatrics. Reproduced by permission.

major network newscasts have shown that crime and violent world events are among the most frequently covered topics. Much of the major national and international news content at the past few years, such as the school shootings, the Oklahoma City bombing, kidnappings of children, reports of ethnic cleansing in Yugoslavia and Kosovo, terror in the Middle East and African countries, the September 11th attacks, and, most recently, "operation Iraqi freedom," contained elements that could well affect children, either because they involved victims or situations that children could easily identify with or because they provided recurring and sometimes even glamorized images of weapons and war.

Real Violence

Although most television news programs are clearly not intended for a child audience, children depend heavily on television for their knowledge about news events and they watch more news broadcasts than many parents and other caregivers might think they do. Most children in the highest grades of elementary school watch the news at least several times a week and even many 3- to 8-year-olds regularly watch television news. Many older elementary school children claim that they watch the news because they find it important to stay informed, but even if children do not choose to watch the news themselves, they still are frequently confronted with it when they are looking for other programs or when their parents are watching. Survey research has shown that about one quarter of US children have a television set in their own bedroom and that in a substantial number of homes, television is turned on all day. With the rise of television channels and Internet services that broadcast news around the clock and with the growing practice of interrupting other television programming to report on "breaking news stories," children of all ages thus may be regularly confronted with highly distressing and violent accounts of murders, catastrophic accidents, war, and other suffering.

It is interesting, however, that the enormous amount of public concern and research effort that has been directed at the prevalence of media violence and at the harmful effects that it may have on children thus far largely has ignored the regularity of real-life violence depicted in television news. For example, the large-scale content analyses of media violence that were specifically aimed at detecting harmful television content for children all excluded from their analyses broadcast news programs. Second, the legislative proposals that have been put forward to protect children from violent media content all disregard television news. Thus, far, there has been no serious discussion about prohibiting television news during "family viewing hours" or about providing a warning before news programs. In addition, the television parental guidelines (V-chip ratings), which were the result of the 1996 Telecommunications Act, are not applied to news and sports programs. The American Academy of Pediatrics is one of the most active professional organizations when it comes to focusing public attention on unhealthy media environments for children and on advocating media education. Nevertheless, in its publications, the American Academy of Pediatrics thus far also focused primarily on preventing the harmful effects of fictional violence. Although that focus should be continued, it should be supplemented with a more in-depth discussion of the potential negative outcomes of real violence portrayed in news programs.

Effects of News Exposure

Research suggest that realism is an important contextual feature of media violence. Studies have shown that more realistic portrayals of violence may heighten levels of involvement and aggression, immediate fright reactions, fear of the world as a scary place, and desensitization, particularly in older, school-aged children, who are able to distinguish the real from the unreal on television. Given the inherent realistic nature of news violence and given other researchers' observations that television news is becoming increasingly sensational and graphic, there is reason to assume that violence in television news has the same impact on children as violence portrayed in fictional television.

Thus far, a handful of studies have specifically investigated the harmful effects that violence portrayed in news broadcasts may have on children. Some of these studies investigated children's reactions to specific events, such as the explosion of the Challenger, or children's reactions to news coverage of the first Gulf War. These studies revealed that many children experienced fairly strong and enduring emotional reactions as a result of their exposure to these news contents. In addition, studies of children's emotional reactions to news about the September 11th terrorist attacks showed that the majority of children experienced profound stress reactions, even if they were not geographically affected by the attacks, and that in some cases these disturbances could lead to posttraumatic stress disorders. Apart from these investigations, several recent studies have shown that the harmful effects of news content are not limited to major catastrophic incidents. In general, these studies indicated that many elementary school children sometimes experience fear in reaction to regular news, such as reports of crime, natural disasters, and "ordinary" plane or traffic accidents, and that 10% to 20% of the children described their feelings as intense to very intense.

Adopt A Broader Conception of Violence

Although all of the above-mentioned studies showed that violence in television news may affect a considerable proportion of the child audience and could lead to serious health effects for certain subgroups of children, their investigations were limited to the effect of violent news content on children's direct frights and their fears of being victimized. It could be that reactions such as stress, frights and worries, and associated effects such as sleep disturbances or nightmares are the most prevailing negative effects of violent news consumption. However, other important effects that are usually associated only with violent entertainment content are conceivable as well.

First, short term aggressive behavior, which is fostered by arousal processes and imitation of violence, could be encouraged by violent news portrayals, especially when news pictures show sensational images of weapons and actually occurring violence. In addition, frequent watching of news programs that overemphasize crime, terror, and war could enhance long-term observational learning of violent schemas or scripts. As has been found for fictional violence, news presentations that are skewed toward violence could encourage people to believe that the world is a hostile place. As a consequence, children could get the impression that violence is a justified means to protect oneself or to resolve conflict. Last, on the basis of the various studies that have demonstrated desensitization effects after repeated exposure to dramatized violence, frequent viewing of real-life violence in news programs could also make young viewers less sensitive to other people's distress and more accepting of violent behavior.

Despite the evident importance of teaching children to become critical viewers of violence in entertainment programs, health care professionals and parents thus also should emphasize the potential negative effects of real violence portrayed in news programs. To understand fully such harmful news contents, however, we should adopt a broader conception of media violence than thus far has been used in the debate about fictional violence.

Physical and Emotional Consequences

The vast amount of research that investigated the prevalence and harmful effects at mediated violence is based on a definition at (fictional) media violence that encompasses the threat, actual use, or physically harmful consequences of violent behavior that is committed by individuals and that is deliberately intended to inflict harm on animate beings. Especially in the case of news content, one needs to conclude that such a notion of violence is too narrow, because it excludes 1) the emotionally harmful consequences of violence; 2) all accidents and natural disasters; 3) any violence that is related to political or economic structure, for which no individual perpetrator can be discerned (eg. war and hunger): and 4) violence directed at inanimate objects or property (eg. vandalism, plundering).

In the case of news content, including the emotionally hurtful outcomes of violence is important because news practitioners are often unable to witness an actual violent event and therefore supplement their stories with images of the physical or emotional results of the violent incident. Because research has shown that not only the physical consequences, such as blood or dead bodies, but also the emotional results, such as people screaming or crying, may seriously affect children, both types of consequences should be included when identifying harmful news content for children. Showing the harmful consequences of violence may have different effects. On the one hand, it may increase fear reactions, especially when children identify with the victims. On the other hand, however, the conveyance of realistic harm and pain cues may decrease aggression and desensitization in children.

Effects of Unintended Violence

When looking at the nature of violence, unintended and structural violence could not be disregarded when identifying harmful news content for children. The traditional restricted focus on intentional harm probably lies in the fact that studies on fictional violence were predominantly linked to the effects of media violence on aggression. However, when other conceivable effects such as immediate fear, fear of being victimized, or desensitization are considered, it is likely that unintended violence such as accident or natural disasters, and structural violence, such as war and human suffering, also affect children. For example, studies on news-induced fright reactions have shown that children of 7 to 8 years of age are almost as frightened by fires and accidents as they are by intended interpersonal violence. In addition, the most recent events related to the second Gulf War underscore the importance of including war and suffering into a conception of media violence. Apart from leading to general fear reactions, images of war could increase aggression in children, especially when actual violent incidents are conveyed without showing the harmful results of those actions. For example, the novel practice during several of the army attacks in Iraq of filming ongoing violence with cameras that were positioned on military vehicles could contribute to the glorification of violence and weapons.

Finally, when looking at the target of violence, it seems reasonable to include not only violence that is directed at animate beings but also violence that is directed at inanimate objects or property. It is interesting that vandalism was not included in previous, notions of harmful media content. However, it is conceivable that, apart from frequent viewing of interpersonal violence, repealed exposure to vandalism enhances aggression and desensitization, because it may increase imitation of destructive behavior and could make viewers more accepting of such conduct.

Enhancing Awareness

Step by step, as children grow up, they should be made aware of problems in the world around them. Although children may get information about human or political crises from different sources, the news media are their main resource for such knowledge. On the positive side, the news media thus could contribute to children's political socialization and prepare them for potential dangers. However, with today's increasing focus on sensationalist and violent news stories and with the thing practice of blurring entertainment and news genres, caregivers should be alerted that most news presentations are not adapted to children's cognitive level and emotional experiences. Pediatricians are in a good position to inform parents, educators, policy makers, and braodcasters of the potential harmful effect of violent news and to suggest ways to enhance children's understanding of such news information. Pediatricians could take action within their own practice, for example by including news consumption in the assessment of children's media histories and by preventing children from watching violent news during their stay in hospital. However, they could also enhance awareness of the negative consequences of violent news within other domains.

First, families and schools should be informed about the potential negative effect of news violence for children. Pediatricians could advise parents and educators to teach children that news is not merely informational or educational but that it could paint an inaccurate picture of the prevalence and meaning of crime and crises and that selection of news topics is often based on the availability of sensational and graphic pictures. Parents should be advised to monitor their children's new consumption. In general, one could say that news programs that are produced for adult audiences are not suitable for children who are younger than 8 years. In addition, if (older) children do watch the news, then they should do so selectively and together with a parent or a school-teacher who could mediate the messages. Parents and educators could lessen the potential negative effects of violent news presentations by making children more critical of news violence. In addition, they could teach children how to cope with anxieties that are induced by news violence, for example by reassuring them that the violent event is not likely to affect their own lives or by providing a better framework to understand the information presented.

Public Debate & Possibilities

Second, pediatricians could enhance public debate about the suitability of television news for children. Thus far, inclusion of news in the media violence debate has been problematic, in part because it would include a discussion about the (il)legitimacy of structural violence committed by states (eg, war) on a more political or sociological level, but for the most part because news program makers need to keep their journalistic independence. For example, regular news programs were purposely excluded from the content analyses in the National Television Violence Studies because the television industry would agree to participate in the studies only if news were disregarded. Pediatricians, however, could make clear that they realize that the public needs to be informed about problems in the world but that at the same time they plea for more awareness of the potential negative effects of news violence, especially on children, and that they want to draw attention to how violent news is broadcast. Studies that have investigated a public health approach to the reporting of violence in news programs have shown that providing a better contextual framework for violence and crime within a news item (eg, by using thematic coverage rather than episodic coverage, by providing risk factors and causal information) decreases the negative effects of news violence in adults. Pediatricians could advocate that such an approach would be beneficial to both children and adults. In addition, considering that almost every news broadcast contains at least 1 violent item, they could encourage a standard rating for news programs that expresses the need for parental guidance for young children.

Third and related to the previous point, pediatricians could promote alternative, special news programs that are tailored to the needs of child audiences. Although a few stations in the United States produce special children's news shows, there is no nationwide daily news program that makes the main news comprehensible to young viewers. In several European countries, such a program does exist. Especially in the United Kingdom and The Netherlands, the public broadcasting cooperations have >20 years of experience with producing a highly professional 15 minutes news program that is broadcast daily in the early evening hours for children aged 8 to 12. Both programs are linked to their adult counterparts, and although they also present special chilren's topics, most of their time is devoted to covering the main national and international news events. Thus, unavoidably, the children news covers violence and crime. However, to offset possible harmful effets of violent news topics, the producers usually apply several "consolation strategies." For example, they ask experts to explain the events in a reassuring manner, they avoid overt graphic film footage, and they do not use additional set or background sounds, such as people screaming or melo-dramatic music. Research has shown that most British and Dutch children prefer to watch the special children's news shows, that they learn much from the information presented and that they are less negatively affected by violent news presented in these programs than by presentations of the same news in programs that are intended for an adult audience.

Promote Research

Finally, pediatricians could promote research into the harmful effects of violent news presentations. Thus far, little to no research attention has been paid to the influence of violent news content on important issues such as 1) children's admiration for weapons and violence, 2) their ideas about violence as a justified means to resolve conflict, 3) their estimates of the amount of violence in real life and estimates of then chance of becoming a victim, 4) their habituation and desensitization toward violence, or 5) their coping with fears and worries induced by violent news content. These issues warrant interdisciplinary attention of media researchers, developmental psychologist, and health care specialists. Unlike most researchers in other disciplines, pediatricians are able to translate scientific result directly into functional advice.

The Public Must Move from Awareness to Action

Elizabeth Thoman

This article by Elizabeth Thoman offers an overview of the media violence debate and some recommendations for how to meet the challenges inherent in the issue. She states that it is time for the American public to move from awareness of the problem to action in the form of a national movement.

Thoman maintains that media violence reinforces the myths and attitudes of what she deems a "culture of violence." Although she thinks it is unrealistic to eradicate violence in the media completely, she does believe that the degree and extent of violence in the media can and should be reduced. The author indicates that the "circle of blame" over the past four decades has resulted in a great deal of talk but little action. In Thoman's view, there is no one solution to the problem of violence in the media. However, a combination of parental and entertainment industry responsibility, as well as media literacy education and political engagement, are steps in the right direction.

Thoman founded Media & Values *magazine as well as the Center for Media Literacy. She is also a founding board member of the Alliance for a Media Literate America (AMLA).*

When Dr. Deborah Prothrow-Stith, assistant dean of Harvard University's School of Public Health, begins one of her speeches on the growing crisis of violence in society, she often tells the story of a young gunshot victim she treated in a Boston hospital emergency room. He expressed surprise that his wound actually hurt.

"I thought, boy, he's really stupid, anybody knows that if you get shot, it's going to hurt. But then it dawned on me that

Elizabeth Thoman, "Media Violence: What if We Changed the Question?" *Center for Media Literacy*, 2002. www.medialit.org/reading_room/article16.html. Copyright © 2002–2007 by Center for Media Literacy. Republished with permission of Center for Media Literacy, conveyed through Copyright Clearance Center, Inc.

on television, when the superhero gets shot in the arm, he uses that arm to hold onto a truck going 85 miles an hour around a corner. He overcomes the driver and shoots a couple of dozen people while he's at it."

Violence as a Way of Life

For decades, the media industry has been trying to tell us that the violence seen on TV and in movies also doesn't hurt, that is, that despite its glamour and impact, it plays no role in making a more violent society.

This is not to say that violence on the screen is the sole cause of violence in the streets. But media violence does reinforce the myths and images, beliefs and attitudes of a culture of violence. It is a messenger for violence as a way of life.

Even if we don't become more aggressive ourselves, we are all affected by the way others behave toward us. And by seeing violence over and over, we also learn to accept and tolerate violence as "the way things are."

At the very least, media violence influences our kids (and us, too) by modeling and glamorizing the use of deadly force as a first choice to solve conflict between characters.

We will never totally eradicate violence from our lives or from the media. That is unrealistic. As long as there are human beings on earth, there will be violence among some of them. But enough questions present themselves about the cumulative impact of violence as entertainment (ie. violence portrayed without consequences or violence as funny) in television, movies, videogames, music and even advertising, that I believe we must, as parents and teachers, as citizens and community leaders, look more closely at the issue of media violence and find ways to reduce it, especially in the lives of our children.

Circle of Blame

No responsible person advocates that violence in the media is desirable. So how does it happen that the media continue to be filled with escalating amounts of violent imagery?

One reason is that for 40 years, American society has been engaged in a "circle of blame" about media violence. The "circle of blame" results from a complicated web of ratings and economics that combine to create a system in which each party feels powerless because "somebody else" has created the problem and, therefore, "somebody else" should solve it:

- Viewers blame those who write and create the shows;

- Writers/directors say the producers require violence in programs in order to get them financed;

- Producers blame network executives for demanding "action" in order to get ratings.

- Network executives say competition is brutal and blame the advertisers for pulling out unless a show gets high ratings;

- Advertisers say it's all up to the viewers!

Easy to Deny the Problem

Another reason is that for those same 40 years, the "circle of blame" has been fueled by one unanswerable question: Does watching violence cause someone to become violent?

Although there is clear evidence that some children imitate Ninja kicks and that occasionally someone will "copycat" a crime seen in the media, we all know from personal reflection that for most viewers most of the time, the watching of violence does not itself cause people to commit criminal violence—or we would all be murderers!

Thus it is easy to deny that media violence is a problem. And it is easy to continue pointing fingers, waiting for "somebody else" to "do something."

But suppose we asked different questions? What if we asked: what does watching violence—over many years—do to our minds? To our hearts? Yes, to our souls? Is the long-term cumulative impact of violence as entertainment transforming our personal worldview? Our collective psyche as a community and as a nation?

Children have always learned how to be and behave as adults from the stories of their childhood. Mass media today are society's storytellers. What kinds of stories are we entertaining our children with? Most importantly, what values and world views do these stories communicate?

In the past two decades we have become deeply concerned about the physical environment we are passing on to our children. The cultural and spiritual environment they are inheriting is equally, if not more, important.

Challenge and Responsibility

It is these questions that now challenge us today as individuals, as parents and as a society. And it is these questions that can help us break the "circle of blame" by encouraging each of us to accept responsibility for reducing media violence wherever we are. What can we do? Here are five ideas.

1. *Parental/adult responsibility for managing media in the lives of children is fundamental.* Parent/teacher organizations, churches, libraries and community groups that sponsor classes and programs to help parents learn to set and enforce age-appropriate viewing standards provide a valuable service for families—and society. When children watch less television, they will see less violence. Young fathers, uncles and older brothers especially need to get the message that too much media violence can truly harm children. Most violent media is targeted at adult males, 18–49. They must be challenged to examine their preference for "action-adventure" especially when children are present.

2. *But parents also have a right to expect that society and its entertainment industries accept responsibility for not*

harming children by allowing the creation of a cultural environment which can endanger children in their formative years. Teddy bears and children's pajamas are subjected to more safety standards than are the TV shows that entertain our children for hours each day. An African proverb states: "It takes a whole village to raise a child." We are all responsible for the cultural environment in which today's children are growing up. That includes the media makers and media owners who control what goes out over the public airwaves or floods our cultural landscape in the images of pop culture. They must behave responsibly as good corporate citizens. And they need to be steadfastly challenged when they do not.

3. *Research indicates that the effects of viewing media violence can be mitigated in all age groups by learning and applying critical viewing and media literacy skills.* Media literacy curricula provide a variety of teaching tools to deconstruct the techniques used to stage violent scenes and decode the various depictions of violence in different media genres—news, cartoons, drama, sports and music. It is important for children to learn early on the difference between reality and fantasy and to know how costumes, camera angles and special effects can fool or mesmerize them. Research shows that critical skills of media analysis can be taught from the earliest years and, through guided practice, can become everyday habits for both children and adults. Media literacy education is a necessary component of violence prevention for young people. It must become a community-wide initiative in cities and towns throughout North America.

4. *There is much denial about the impact of media violence because accepting it as a problem means we might have to make changes in our own lives and values.* Accepting

it as a problem challenges those adults who uncon-
sciously—or consciously—take pleasure in violent entertainment. Accepting it as a problem means we may
have to face the shadow side of our human nature
which most of us want to avoid. Accepting it as a problem means we might have to admit our own complicity
in the greedy callousness that can corrupt the human
spirit. Media critic Elayne Rapping notes that if there is
more media violence today, it's partly because, yes, we
live in a more violent world. But that violent world was
created not so much by Rambo films as by our own
tax dollars which support multinational arms dealers
and international corporations that make billions of
dollars on military technology. Unfortunately there is a
healthy profit to be made by escalating fear and hatred
into ever-more sophisticated ways to maim and destroy
human lives.

5. *Finally, there is no one solution to the problem of media
   violence in our time.* But there are many steps that each
   of us can take, wherever we are, to reduce the amount
   and impact of violent entertainment in our lives and in
   the lives of children. And, as in so many other movements, it is the accumulation of those individual actions that adds up to create an unstoppable force of
   public opinion. "I'm willing to be a pebble," says the
   poster at my nearby Ben & Jerry's, "if I'm also part of
   an avalanche."

From Awareness to Action

We will continue to have a problem with media violence until
a majority of the American public understands why it is harmful and decides to change their own behavior—recognizing
that their behavior, along with others, cumulatively adds up to
widespread social change. Just like we have all come to believe
that every single pop can we pick up is one small step in sav-
ing the environment.

It's time to break the "circle of blame" by engaging millions of people in a national movement that leads from awareness to action, from passivity to engagement, from denial and blame to accepting responsibility for what each of us can do as individuals, as parents, as citizens in today's media society.

Chronology

264 B.C.–404 A.D.
Rome hosts gladiator games, which features combat—usually to the death—of fighters in public arenas, most notable the Colosseum.

1933–35
Payne Fund publishes studies conducted from 1929 to 1932. This series of studies, supported by the Motion Picture Research Council, were designed to study media influence.

1934
The Federal Communications Act is passed in June, establishing the Federal Communications Commission (FCC). The FCC regulates broadcasting.

1952
The House of Representatives Interstate and Foreign Commerce Subcommittee holds a hearing in June on violence in radio and television and its impact on youth. This is the first congressional hearing of its kind.

1956
Researchers conduct a study on children watching violent and non-violent cartoons. The group who watched the violent cartoon were observed afterwards to exhibit a greater likelihood to hit other children and break toys.

1972
The National Institute of Mental Health and the Surgeon General issue a report, the first large-scale government project on the topic, that claims exposure to violence on television fosters aggression in children.

1982

The National Institute of Mental Health issues a ten-year follow-up report to the 1972 study. The report cites a consensus among most of the research community that there is a link between television violence and aggression.

1990

The "Television Violence Act" is signed into law by President George Bush. As a result of this act, the major U.S. networks have three years to curb depictions (via voluntary means) of violence on American television.

1993

A patent for the V-chip is issued January 31 to inventor Tim Collings. The V-chip is designed to screen out violent programming on television.

1995

Congress introduces a pair of bills in June, both of which call for the use of a television program rating system. The bills also require the insertion of V-chip technology into all new televisions.

1995

The UCLA Television Violence Monitoring Report, funded by NBC, CBS, ABC, and Fox is released in September, concluding that violent content has improved, but important concerns remains, such as "sinister combat violence" on Saturday morning TV shows.

1996

President Bill Clinton's January "State of the Union" address confirms his intention to push for the use of V-chip technology. He challenges the entertainment industry to institute a ratings system and calls for a television summit to discuss concrete ways to improve television content.

1996

A new telecommunications bill is passed in February that includes provisions requiring manufacturers to install V-chips. The bill gives the broadcasting industry one year to develop a ratings system. On February 8, President Clinton signs the bill into law.

1997

The television ratings system debuts in January. The ratings appear for 15 seconds in the upper left-hand corner of the screen at the start of each show (with the exception of news and sports).

1999

A study finds that memories of frightening media images continued to disturb a significant number of participants years later: Over 90 percent report they still experience effects, ranging from sleep disturbances to avoidance of certain situations, from images viewed during chidhood.

2001

A study of videogamers reveals that children and young people who play violent video games, even for short periods, are more likely to behave aggressively in real life.

2003

A study reports that violent music lyrics increased aggressive thoughts and hostile feelings among 500 college students.

2003

A Kaiser Family Foundation study found that 47 percent of parents with children between the ages of four and six report that their children have imitated aggressive behaviors they'd seen on TV. The study also found that 87 percent of children mimic positive behaviors.

Organizations to Contact

The editors have compiled the following list of organizations concerned with the issues debated in this book. The descriptions are derived from materials provided by the organizations. All have publications or information available for interested readers. The list was compiled on the date of publication of the present volume; the information provided here may change. Be aware that many organizations take several weeks or longer to respond to inquiries, so allow as much time as possible.

American Civil Liberties Union (ACLU)
125 Broad St., 18th Floor, New York, NY   10004-2400
(212) 549-2500
aclu@aclu.org
www.aclu.org

The ACLU champions the rights set forth in the Declaration of Independence and the Constitution. It opposes the censoring of any form of speech, including media depictions of violence. The ACLU publishes books, handbooks, project reports, pamphlets, and public policy reports. The ACLU website provides access to some of these publications as well as press releases, legal briefs and opinions, and legislative documents, including "Freedom of Expression in the Arts and Entertainment."

American Psychological Association (APA)
Office of Public Affairs, 750 First St. NE
Washington, DC   20002-4242
(202) 336-5700
public.affairs@apa.org
www.apa.org

This society of psychologists aims to "advance psychology as a science, as a profession, and as a means of promoting human welfare." Although the APA opposes censorship, it believes that viewing television violence can have potential dangers for children. On its website the APA provides access to its Adults & Children Together Against Violence program (www.actagainstviolence.com), which includes information on the impact of media violence and suggestions for parents and others who care for children, including the handout "*Strategies to Reduce the Impact of Media Violence in Young Children's Lives.*"

Cato Institute

1000 Massachusetts Ave. NW, Washington, DC 20001
(202) 842-0200 • fax: (202) 842-3490
cato@cato.org
www.cato.org

The institute is a libertarian public policy research foundation dedicated to promoting limited government, individual political liberty, and free-market economics. It publishes the bimonthly Policy Report and the periodic Cato Journal. Cato's website provides access to policy reports, congressional testimony, legal briefs, the current issue and archives of its quarterly, *Regulation*, and articles by Cato analysts, including "Rating Entertainment Ratings: How Well are They Working for Parents, and What Can Be Done to Improve Them?"

Center for Media Literacy (CML)

23852 Pacific Coast Highway, #472, Malibu, CA 90265
(310) 456-1225 • fax: (310) 456-0020
cml@medialit.org
www.medialit.org

CML is an educational organization that provides leadership, public education, and professional development. The organization also provides educational resources and is dedicated to promoting media literacy education as a framework for analyzing and creating media content. CML works nationally to aid people, especially the young, develop critical thinking and media production skills. The goal of CML is to make wise media choices possible.

Federal Communications Commission (FCC)

1919 M St. NW, Washington, DC 20554
(888) CallFCC (225-5322)
fccinfo@fcc.gov
www.fcc.gov

The FCC is an independent government agency responsible for regulating telecommunications. It develops and implements policy concerning interstate and international communications by radio, television, wire, satellite, and cable. The FCC is required to review the educational programming efforts of the networks. It publishes various reports, updates, and reviews that can be accessed on-line at their website.

Media Awareness Network (MNet)

1500 Merivale Rd., 3rd floor, Ottawa, Ontario K2E 6Z5
  Canada
(613) 224-7721 • fax: (613) 224-1958
info@media-awareness.ca
www.media-awareness.ca

MNet is a web-based project that houses a comprehensive collection of media education and Internet literacy resources. A Canadian non-profit organization, MNet began in 1996 and aims to promote critical thinking in young people about media. In addition, the organization creates online awareness programs, conducts workshops, and offers resources such as lesson plans for teachers and reference materials for students and parents.

Media Coalition

139 Fulton St., Suite 302, New York, NY 10038
(212) 587-4025
mediacoalition@mediacoalition.org
www.mediacoalition.org

The Media Coalition defends the First Amendment right to produce and sell books, magazines, recordings, videotapes, and video games. It defends the American public's right to have access to the broadest possible range of opinion and entertainment, including works considered offensive or harmful due to their violent or sexually explicit content. It opposes the government-mandated ratings system for television. On its website, the coalition provides legislative updates and access to reports, including *Shooting the Messenger: Why Censorship Won't Stop Violence.*

National Coalition Against Censorship (NCAC)
275 Seventh Ave., New York, NY   10001
(212) 807-6222
ncac@ncac.org
www.ncac.org

The NCAC is an alliance of national non-profit organizations, including literary, artistic, religious, educational, professional, labor, and civil liberties groups. The coalition is united by a conviction that freedom of thought, inquiry, and expression must be defended. The NCAC work to educate members and the public at large about the dangers of censorship and how to oppose them. Its website provides access to press releases, legal briefs, and congressional testimony on censorship issues including violence in the media.

National Center for Children Exposed to Violence (NCCEV)
230 South Frontage Road, P.O. Box 207900
New Haven, CT   06520-7900
(877) 49 NCCEV (496-2238)
colleen.vadala.@yale.edu

The NCCEV was established in 1999 at the Yale Child Study Center by the U.S. Department of Justice. The NCCEV's mission is to increase the capacity of individuals and communities to reduce the incidence and impact of violence on children and families. It also trains and supports the professionals who provide intervention and treatment to children and families affected by violence. The organization aims to increase professional and public awareness of the effects of violence—including media violence—on children, families, communities, and society.

The National Institute on Media and Family

606 24th Ave. South, Suite 606, Minneapolis, MN   55454
(612) 672-5437 (voice) • fax: (612) 672-4113
www.mediafamily.org

Founded in 1996, the National Institute on Media and the Family is a leading research-based organization that investigates the positive and harmful effects of media on children and youth. It is an independent, nonpartisan, nonsectarian, and nonprofit organization that focuses on research, education, and advocacy. The organization's MediaWise® movement helps families make wiser media choices and encourages parents to monitor what their children watch.

The UNESCO International Clearinghouse on Children, Youth and Media

Nordicom, Goteborg University, Box 713
Goteborg SE 405 30
   Sweden
nordicom@nordicom.gu.se
www.nordicom.gu.se

The clearinghouse disseminates information about the relationship between young people and media violence, alternatives to media violence, and efforts to reduce violence in the media. It publishes a yearbook and *Influence of Media Violence: A Brief Research Summary*. On its website, UNESCO provides access to its database and current and past issues of its newsletter, *News on Children and Violence on the Screen*.

For Further Research

Books

M. Barker and J. Petley, *Ill Effects: The Media/Violence Debate*. New York: Routledge, 2001.

J.L. Freedman, *Media Violence and Its Effects on Aggression: Assessing the Scientific Evidence*. Toronto: University of Toronto Press, 2002.

D.A. Gentile, *Media Violence and Children*. Westport, CT: Praeger, 2003.

J.H. Goldstein, *Sports Violence*. New York: Springer-Verlag, 1983.

———— *Why We Watch: The Attractions of Violent Entertainment*. New York: Oxford University Press, 1998.

D. Grossman, *Stop Teaching Our Kids to Kill: A Call to Action against TV, Movie, and Video Game Violence*. New York: Crown, 1999.

G. Jones, *Killing Monsters: Why Children Need Fantasy, Super Heroes and Make-Believe Violence*. New York: Basic Books, 2002.

M. Kieran, *Media Ethics: A Philosophical Approach*. Westport, CT: Praeger, 1997.

S.J. Kirsh, *Children, Adolescents, and Media Violence: A Critical Look at the Research*. Thousand Oaks, CA: Sage, 2006.

T.G. Moeller, *Youth Aggression and Violence: A Psychological Approach*. Mahwah, NJ: Erlbaum, 2001.

W.J. Potter, *The 11 Myths about Media Violence*. Thousand Oaks, CA: Sage, 2002.

H. Schechter, *Savage Pastimes: A Cultural History of Violent Entertainment.* New York: St. Martin's Press, 2005.

M. Shaw, *Civil society and Media in Global Crises: Representing Distant Violence.* New York: Pinter, 1996.

K. Sternheimer, *It's Not the Media: The Truth About Pop Culture's Influence on Children.* Boulder, CO: Westview, 2003.

D. Trend, *The Myth of Media Violence: A Critical Introduction.* Boston: Blackwell, 2006.

Periodicals

J. Alter, "Moving Beyond the Blame Game," *Newsweek*, vol. 133, no. 30, May 17, 1999.

C.A. Anderson, L. Berkowitz, E. Donnerstein, R.L. Huesmann, J.D. Johnson, Linz, et al., "The Influence of Media Violence on Youth," *Psychological Science in the Public Interest*, 2003.

C.A. Anderson, N. Carnagey, and J. Eubanks, "Exposure to Violent Media: The Effects of Songs with Violent Lyrics on Aggressive Thoughts and Feelings," *Journal of Personality and Social Psychology*, 2003.

P. Arriaga, F. Esteves, P. Carneiro, and M.B. Monteiro, "Violent Computer Games and Their Effects on State Hostility and Physiological Arousal," *Aggressive Behavior*, 2006.

B.D. Bartholow, B.J. Bushman, and M.A. Sestir, "Chronic Violent Video Game Exposure and Desensitization to Violence: Behavioral and Event-Related Brain Potential Data," *Journal of Experimental Social Psychology*, 2006.

L.R. BeVier, "Controlling Communications That Teach or Demonstrate Violence: The Movie Made Them Do It," *Journal of Law, Medicine, and Ethics*, 2004.

M. Buijzen, J.H. Van der Molen, and P. Sondij, "Parental Mediation of Children's Emotional Responses to a Violent News Event," *Communication Research*, 2007.

B.A. Bushman and C.A. Anderson, "Media Violence and the American Public: Scientific Fact Versus Media Misinformation," *American Psychologist*, 2001.

E.K. Carll, "News Portrayal of Violence and Women: Implications for Public Policy," *American Behavioral Scientist*, 2003.

T.L. Cheng, R.A. Brenner, J.L. Wright, H.C. Sachs, P. Moyer, and M.R. Rao, "Children's Violent Television Viewing: Is Anyone Watching?" *Pediatrics*, 2004.

R.R. Dalal, "Congress Shall Make No Law Abridging Freedom of Speech—Even if It Causes Our Children to Kill?" *Seton Hall Legislative Journal*, 2001.

J. Deselms and J. Altman, "Immediate and Prolonged Effects of Videogame Violence," *Journal of Applied Social Psychology*, 2003.

R.H. DuRant, M. Rich, S.J. Emans, E.S. Rome, E. Allred, and E.R. Woods, "Violence and Weapon Carrying in Music Videos: A Content Analysis," *Archives of Pediatrics & Adolescent Medicine*, 1997.

V. Juluri, "Nonviolence and Media Studies," *Communication Theory*, 2005.

M. Muscari, "Media Violence: Advice for Parents," *Pediatric Nursing*, 2002.

C. Olson, "Media Violence Research and Youth Violence Data: Why Do They Conflict?" *Academic Psychiatry*, 2004.

A.L.S. Risner, "Violence, Minors and the First Amendment: What Is Unprotected Speech and What Should Be?" *Saint Louis University Public Law Review*, 2005.

M.D. Slater, "Alienation, Aggression, and Sensation Seeking as Predictors of Adolescent Use of Violent Film, Computer, and Website Content," *Journal of Communication*, 2003.

B.K. Smith, "The Fight over Video Game Violence: Recent Developments in Politics, Social Science, and Law," *Law and Psychology Review*, 2006.

D. Zillmann and J.B. Weaver "Aggressive Personality Traits in the Effects of Violent Imagery on Unprovoked Impulsive Aggression," *Journal of Research in Personality*, 2007.

Index